THE CONFIDENCE COACH

RV

Lisa Phillips is one of Australia's most inspiring empowerment experts. Originally from the UK, she founded her 'Amazing Coaching' business in 2001, after working in over 20 countries in senior management positions before deciding to follow her true passion and re-train as a coach and confidence expert. Lisa appears regularly on television, shares her advice in many business and lifestyle magazines and has been interviewed on numerous international radio shows. She has her own 'Confidence Coaching' column in the UK press, while her popular 'Spiritual and Irritable' radio show attracts both national and international self-development guests. Lisa is regularly asked to speak at large events in both the private and public sector. With her warm sense of humour and genuine, open style, Lisa inspires people to increase their confidence, stop being their own worst enemy, and trigger lasting change in their lives — while enjoying themselves at the same time! In 2014 Lisa received the bronze Stevie Award for Women in Business.

THE CONFIDENCE COACH

Take control of your life and wellbeing

LISA PHILLIPS

EXISLE
PUBLISHING

'Thanks to Lisa Phillips' wisdom and the examples that live among the pages of her book, you will begin to see a wonderful glimmer of growth, confidence and fulfillment. You will want to pass this gem on to your friends, clients and family. I'm excited to see how this important writing will change your life!'

— Dianne Schwartz, author of *Whose Face is in the Mirror?*

'*The Confidence Coach* is the perfect companion for anyone who wishes to increase their confidence levels easily from the inside out — without struggle. Not only does this book include simple and practical ways to feel good, but it also supports the reader to understand what may have been holding them back in the past from being a confident person. Lisa has an approach to confidence which is leading edge, and I know from personal experience that it works! I have had the opportunity to see her work with people personally and was blown away by her expertise and passion in the field of confidence building.'

— Dani Pola, founder of The Self Esteem Team, breakfast announcer on Southern Cross Radio Australia

'To understand other people, we need to understand ourselves. Lisa — having trained under the world's leading self-development experts — has remarkable insight into human nature and how we can become masters of our own destinies. Under Lisa's umbrella are presented many aspects of mind, including negativity, worrying, safe personal boundaries, developing confidence in ourselves, in public speaking, in relationships and in our career, and, above all, taking back our own power. *The Confidence Coach* is a virtual manual for enhancing quality of life through developing confidence in ourselves and in what we do.'

— Roger French, health director and editor, Natural Health Society of Australia

'*The Confidence Coach* presents a prescription for increasing confidence with doses that go down easy. It asks the questions you may wish you'd asked yourself. Don't miss out on discovering your answers!'

—Patricia Evans, author of *The Verbally Abusive Relationship*

'*The Confidence Coach* is really like having your own personal coach encouraging you and guiding you toward greater self-confidence. In an easy-to-read format Lisa presents a step-by-step process that has proven successful for many, many people. She presents powerful action steps to help you with such confidence-robbing issues as negative self-talk and worrying about what other people think. One of her most powerful strategies is to help people to be kinder and more accepting of themselves.'

— Beverly Engel, LMFT, psychotherapist and bestselling author of 21 self-help books

'Have you ever struggled a little or a lot with your feelings of confidence? Lisa offers an easy-to-read and practical guide to help you learn how to flex your "confidence muscle". She clearly shows you how to navigate difficult situations, feel better about yourself and be a confident and assertive person. Lisa is a trusted authority in the field of confidence and personal empowerment and I'm so delighted she has written this book so even more people have access to her knowledge and toolkit of resources. Lisa will inspire you to feel better about yourself with her excellent guidance in this lighthearted and reader-friendly resource.'

— Stacey Ashley, PCC Coach, ICF Australia; managing director, Ashley Coaching & Consulting

First published 2015

Exisle Publishing Pty Ltd
'Moonrising', Narone Creek Road, Wollombi, NSW 2325, Australia
P.O. Box 60–490, Titirangi, Auckland 0642, New Zealand
www.exislepublishing.com

A CiP record for this book is available from the National Library of
Australia.

ISBN 978-1-921966-74-3

Designed by Big Cat Design
Typeset in Minion Pro 11.45 on 17.5pt
Printed in China

This book uses paper sourced under ISO 14001 guidelines from
well-managed forests and other controlled sources.

10 9 8 7 6 5 4 3 2 1

Disclaimer
While this book is intended as a general information resource
and all care has been taken in compiling the contents, this book
does not take account of individual circumstances and is not in
any way a substitute for professional advice. Neither the author
nor the publisher and their distributors can be held responsible
for any loss, claim or action that may arise from reliance on the
information contained in this book.

*To my wonderful clients, for continuing to inspire me;
and also to my internal guidance system, for always
pointing me in the right direction.*

contents

PART ONE

Setting Key Foundations for Long-Term Confidence

INTRODUCTION

WHERE HAS MY CONFIDENCE GONE?

Unless I am very much mistaken, you have picked up this book because you feel that in some way your life lacks that illusive magic ingredient: confidence.

Well, the good news is that you have arrived at the right place. As an experienced confidence coach, I have worked with thousands of men and women from a wide range of cultures and backgrounds, and I am delighted to inform you that, by completing the simple tips in this book, you, like thousands of others around the globe, will easily learn to build up what I call your 'confidence muscle' so that it grows to be a strong and healthy part of your life.

I like to define confidence as a muscle because just like any other muscle in our body, confidence needs time and encouragement to grow and strengthen. It is not something that instantly gains strength overnight, but with consistent and steady care it will become a healthy and embedded part of who you are. Gaining confidence is a life-altering journey; you can gain so much just by making small adjustments to your thought processes and behaviours.

I am well aware that your confidence muscle may not have had a very good start in life, or that it might have been crushed over the years — but from this moment on, you can learn to strengthen this muscle and consequently become a more confident, calm and courageous person.

I suffered from low self-confidence until I hit my mid-thirties. As a child I was bullied at school and as an adult I encountered bullying behaviour from a manager at work. I also spent far too long in an unhealthy relationship I didn't have the confidence to leave. All these experiences led to me feeling frustrated and angry with myself for allowing other people to walk all over me and take advantage of my 'nice' nature. The occasional   beating myself up and generally believing that everyone else in the world was somehow better than me, I took that all-important first step into nourishing and building my own inner confidence muscle. Thankfully, I have never looked back, and for the past twelve years in my role as a confidence coach I have helped other people to build up their very own strong confidence muscle.

Today I would like to accompany you on your own exciting journey into confidence. To ensure that your confidence muscle builds from a solid foundation, I have structured this book into three key parts.

In Part One we will focus on the psychological reasons for low self-confidence, such as negative beliefs and past programming. In doing this, we ensure that we set a firm foundation on which to build. This includes identifying any old self-talk or programming and uncovering some of the potential blockages that unconsciously prevent you from being confident. By focusing on these areas first, your journey into confidence will also feel much easier.

In Part Two we will take a more hands-on approach, in which I will share some exercises to help you build confidence from the inside out. These include setting confidence goals and creating a vision of a confident life.

Finally, in Part Three, we will concentrate on specific areas in which you might need an extra confidence boost, such as in relationships or career.

In each of these three parts you will also find case studies and quotations from some of my clients. Not only are these a valuable resource, but they will also provide you with reassurance that you are not alone in this journey. Please ensure that you have a journal to hand when working through each section, so you can take notes or write your answers to the questions raised.

This book is not supposed to be a struggle or hard work — particularly if you follow each of the sections in order. With this in mind, my aim for each and every reader is not only to develop and maintain a strong confidence muscle, but to also have fun while building it!

CHAPTER 1

THE CONFIDENCE MUSCLE

We each have a unique definition of what confidence means to us. For some, it is the ability to stand up in public and speak with ease, and for others, it may be simply walking into a crowded room without feeling awkward or blushing from head to toe. It also could be as basic as comfortably getting naked in front of our partner with the lights on, or having the confidence to go out and land a great new job. Confidence really is different for everyone and can be influenced by our background, beliefs and expectations.

The consistent thing about confidence (or should I say a lack of it) is that it often holds us back from living the life we really want. It can prevent us from asking for that pay rise, leaving work on time, starting our own business or even getting out and about on the dating scene again after a divorce. Worst of all, it can leave us feeling inadequate and frustrated for not having the nerve to go out and do what we really want to do.

CINDY

Cindy loved to dance. During an international trip she was introduced to a new exercise-dance style that she knew would be popular in her home country.

Although Cindy was an accomplished dancer, she was terrified of standing up in front of other people and actually teaching a dance class. This greatly frustrated her because deep down she knew how successful she could be, but every time she thought about it her fears would creep in, telling her that she wasn't confident enough to do it and that she would only make a fool of herself. Imagine her disappointment when a year later, one of her colleagues introduced the same dance style to her local gym and it became an overnight success!

An interesting point about confidence is that it is not necessarily a general characteristic that impacts every single area of our life. Many people feel confident in a few parts of their life but may struggle in a specific area. For example, you could feel very confident at work but suffer from anxiety and nerves when dealing with your personal relationships. For others, low self-confidence may be something that impacts life in general. The good news is that whatever your personal confidence situation, general or specific, you can improve it.

One of the saddest things I see is people holding the belief that everyone else around them is far more confident than they are. This idea is too prevalent in our society today and we spend wasted hours comparing ourselves to other people or beating ourselves up for not being brave or good enough. It is as if we think we have missed the confidence bus and are doomed to spend a life watching everyone else enjoying it! This issue has been heightened in recent years due to the impact of social media, where it becomes all too easy to compare our lives to those 'perfect' profiles that we see each day on social-media platforms. Many of us take in this information we see online as being 100 per cent factual, which can lead to us unfavourably comparing ourselves to others and feeling that we have fallen short in our own lives.

I will let you in on a little secret, though: this really isn't the case. Deep down every one of us has fears and will suffer from a lack of confidence at some time in our life — but we can learn to deal with it.

> **'As soon as I talk to an attractive man, I just freeze up.**
> **My heart starts beating fast and I just know that I am not**
> **going to have anything valuable to say.' Jane, 25**

WHERE DOES OUR CONFIDENCE COME FROM?

Unfortunately, many of us have been led to believe that our confidence comes from other people. As a result, we often point the blame finger at others for 'failing' to instil in us the confidence we desire. In addition, we blame other people for shattering our confidence into little pieces.

The real truth is that you get your confidence from YOU, not from other people. It is purely an internal process. Okay, I acknowledge that many of us would like to have learned more about being self-assured when we were growing up, but hey, you are an adult now, so you can choose to take responsibility — today. It doesn't matter how long you have felt lacking in confidence, you can make a decision right now to do something positive about it, and I will show you how.

Don't forget that within every one of us lies a confidence muscle. Yes, it may have been downtrodden and crushed over the years, but that confidence muscle is still inside you and nobody can take it away — unless you let them. Just like any other muscle, it needs regular exercise to get it working effectively again.

Before we move into the next chapter, please stop for a few minutes and take the time to write down the answers to the following questions.

The first question will help you examine the ways in which low self-confidence has been affecting your life to date. The second question will help you gain clarity on what may happen if you don't decide to do something about it. Please remember that there is never a wrong or right answer to any of the questions or steps contained in this book; just focus on whatever answer feels true for you.

- **How have you let your lack of confidence affect your life?**
- **What will your life be like in five years' time if you do not change?**

We all have access to the confidence muscle and it doesn't matter who you are or how long low self-confidence has been an issue in your life — it can become strong and powerful by following the steps outlined in this book.

TOP TIPS FOR CONFIDENCE

- **Everyone already has some degree of confidence; it may have just been worn down over the years.**
- **Each and every one of us has the ability to build a strong confidence muscle.**
- **If you don't take action now, things may never change.**
- **Building a firm foundation will make your confidence journey far easier and enjoyable.**

CHAPTER 2

NEGATIVE SELF-TALK

To build a firm foundation for confidence, we need to explore the types of thoughts that run through our mind. When these thoughts are predominantly negative, they can cause a blockage to building confidence. Let's begin this process by referring back to Cindy's case study in the previous chapter. We all know that hindsight is a great thing, but can you see how Cindy's negative thought patterns were blocking her from becoming more confident about teaching a dance class?

When Cindy first came to see me, she explained that every time she even considered moving forward and teaching a dance class, her mind became filled with thoughts of discouragement, fear and anxiety. This inner dialogue, or 'self-talk', was causing her to feel so anxious about teaching a class that she often laid awake until the small hours worrying about what could go wrong.

Her internal negative self-talk sounded something like this:

- **I can't do it; I will make a total fool of myself.**

- **What if I forget the moves or get my words all mixed up?**

- **What if people don't like it?**

- **I have always been scared of speaking in front of other people.**

- **I will be so embarrassed if it all goes wrong.**

- **Everyone else is far more confident than I am.**

Let's be honest — where does this negative self-talk come from? Did Cindy hear these words from her friends, family or the people she hoped would attend her class? No. All of these negative thoughts came from inside Cindy's head. Nobody else was thinking them. The majority of these negative thoughts had been part of Cindy's life for so long that she never even considered doubting or questioning them. She simply believed that they were true. Unfortunately, the longer she thought about these things, the greater the fears became in her mind and the more power these thoughts had over her.

Our inner self-talk — the thoughts we choose to think and believe about ourselves — are just old, outdated and worn-out patterns. In fact, research from the National Science Foundation shows that we repeat over 95 per cent of the same thoughts every single day. These repetitive thoughts are merely bad thinking habits, and there is very little evidence to suggest that they are factually true. In fact, all they do is shrivel up our confidence muscle and make it seem more difficult for us to take a risk and do the things we really want to do. The good news is that although your mind may tell you differently, it is fairly easy to learn to change this internal dialogue into a more positive mindset that will assist you to succeed, rather than condemn you to fail.

Do you ever find yourself thinking that you must free yourself of your entire negative self-talk programming before you can achieve a positive mindset? This is a common belief and it is poppycock — if you believe this, you will only drive yourself crazy and find more reasons to beat yourself up. The easiest, simplest and quickest way to create a positive mindset is not to try to delete your negative thoughts, but to simply search for different thoughts, ones that soothe your fears rather than frighten you. When you consciously focus your attention on this, your fears will lose impact and you will end up feeling more relaxed. Imagine how nice it would feel to have your own personal cheerleader, encouraging you to do your best and also soothing you when you feel worried or nervous.

Many of us have been listening to and acting on our negative thoughts for 20-, 30-, 40- or even 50-plus years, so it is important to have patience and not expect to get the hang of it overnight. Just begin by trying to be a little more aware of when your negative thoughts come up to the surface. When you do notice them, consciously choose to focus on, and soothe yourself with, encouraging and gentle thoughts instead. This alone will start the process of building new, positive and confident pathways in your mind and body.

For example, when you notice a negative thought, instead of getting annoyed or angry with yourself, choose a more soothing thought such as, 'It's okay, everything is going to be fine, I don't have to worry about improving all of my negative thoughts right now.'

Think back to when you were a youngster and you first learned to ride a bike. Did you sit on the seat for the first time expecting to fail or worrying about all the things that could go wrong, or did you see it as an opportunity to try something new and think about all the great adventures you could have after mastering the art of bike-riding? Admittedly you may have had a few negative thoughts and worries about hurting yourself, but you didn't let this stop you, did you?

Even if you did end up falling from your bicycle, I am sure you wouldn't have labelled yourself as a failure or completely given up bike-riding for good. Children often have a far more positive mindset than adults — and it is this encouraging and supportive attitude that we need to focus on reproducing as adults, in order to build up our confidence muscle.

ACTION STEP

Make a list of all the thoughts that prevent you from feeling confident. When you have finished, rip the paper into small pieces, then burn it or bury it in your garden. (I know this action step may sound a little bizarre but the simple act of writing down your negative thoughts can help release the power these beliefs have over you. In addition, it often feels really good to see them go up in smoke or hidden away underground for good!)

Let's take a minute to again look back at Cindy in our first case study. Can you imagine how different things may have turned out for Cindy if she had consciously chosen to take a more positive mindset and focused on kind and supportive thoughts that encouraged her to introduce the new dance style? What would have happened if she had simply acknowledged the fact that she was feeling scared but decided to embrace the fear instead of letting it hold her back? What would happen if she decided to encourage herself, soothe her fears and just GO FOR IT!

MARCUS

Let me introduce you to Marcus. Marcus recently became single after a 25-year relationship with his wife ended. When he first came to see me, he was terrified of getting out on the dating scene again and had lost all faith in women. He admitted that his self-talk sounded a bit like this:

- **I haven't got much time for dating and I really don't enjoy it. What's the point?**

- **I always struggle to find something interesting to say around women.**

- **I have put on some weight in the past few years; why would anyone find me attractive?**

- **I haven't dated for ages — I wonder if everything has changed?**

Despite this negative dialogue, Marcus was determined not to let these fears hold him back. Yes, he still felt nervous about getting into the dating scene, but rather than allow these fears to hold him back, he decided to take responsibility and soothe his fears with a more encouraging and confident mindset, allowing him to move into a better-feeling place. His new confident mindset began like this:

'I know that I feel scared and uncomfortable about dating again, but rather than scare myself about it and fill my head with negative thoughts, I am going to encourage myself to do it anyway. Okay, I know that I may feel nervous but rather than focus on this, I am going to start to change my mindset to one that makes me feel better. When I think about it, it would actually be really nice to have a partner in my life again.'

His new self-talk thoughts included:

- **I know I'm not perfect, but hey, I am a good catch!**
- **It will be fine, I can handle it. Things can't have changed that much.**
- **I am going to go into dating with an idea of just having fun — let's face it, I don't need to look at every woman I meet as my new life partner.**
- **This will be really good practice for me.**
- **If I really don't like it, I can always leave.**

Can you see how Marcus has set himself up for success rather than for failure? It is not that he feels completely confident about getting back into dating, but rather than use his thoughts to discourage himself further, he has deliberately chosen to change his mindset to one that will build him up, not knock him down. By doing this, Marcus also feels far more relaxed and has reduced the pressure on himself to find Ms Right.

I can't stress enough the importance of encouraging and soothing yourself into a better-feeling place. You don't even need to know how things will happen; you just need to be willing to hold the hand of fear and choose kind and nourishing thoughts to accompany you on your confidence journey. Also, acknowledge the fact that whenever you do anything new you are going to feel a little uncomfortable and scared, but choose to focus your energy on building yourself up — not putting yourself down.

TOP TIPS FOR A CONFIDENT MINDSET

- **Remember: negative beliefs are merely the lies we choose to believe about ourselves.**

- **Negative self-talk may never disappear, but you can soothe yourself into a better-feeling place.**

- **Decide today not to let old negative thought patterns hold you back any longer.**

- **Acknowledge that you will often feel nervous — but don't let these nerves hold you back from doing what you really want to do.**

- **Encourage yourself with kind words and remind yourself that you are going to be okay.**

- **Don't expect to be perfect first time around!**

- **Always praise yourself when you take action towards building a confident mindset.**

- **Whenever you feel fear, practise a soothing, encouraging dialogue with yourself.**

- **Treat yourself like your own best friend.**

ACTION STEP

Try to become more aware when negative thoughts pop into your head. When you do catch them, practise soothing and encouraging yourself instead. If you can do this once a day, it's a great start, so please don't get annoyed with yourself if it takes a little longer than you would like.

CHAPTER 3

NEGATIVE PROGRAMMING

One of the key reasons for our automatic negative self-talk is the programming we received during childhood. Although we may tell ourselves as adults that we want to become more confident people, sometimes there are deeper childhood beliefs and fears under the surface that need to be healed or brought to the surface first. If we don't work on healing these, they can literally keep us stuck or unknowingly drag us back into old defeating behaviours. These old beliefs and fears are often held deep within our unconscious mind, so an important step in our confidence journey is to start to identify and release this negative programming before it self-sabotages our attempts to feel better.

Let me explain further how this works. When you are born, your brain is basically unprogrammed — like a blank hard disk on a computer or an MP3 player before it is loaded with your favourite tunes.

Just like these electronic items, your childhood brain needed to receive some programming or data before it started to work. Obviously you were too young to program your brain yourself, so the universe kindly organized for this to happen through the people around you such as your friends and family, teachers, religious institutions and the media. Unfortunately, you didn't get much say in the quality of the programming you received. In fact, at this stage, you hadn't even developed a filter to distinguish the difference between accurate data and spam, and you simply accepted without question whatever information or programming you received.

If you were lucky enough to be raised in a family where the majority of your programming was positive, then you will have grown up with a mind filled with positive messages. However, many people are not so lucky and have their brains formatted with other people's negative beliefs and distorted programming. This can take many forms, from general family statements like, 'Don't take risks,' or 'Better to be safe than sorry,' to common phrases such as, 'Don't make a fuss.' If your family didn't have a strong, healthy collective confidence muscle, then chances are you would have heard messages such as, 'Life isn't safe,' or 'You won't be able to do that.' Many people are also raised in unhealthy environments in which they are subjected to taunts or insults such as being called 'fat', 'stupid' or 'unattractive'. In all of these examples, a child simply soaks up this programming as if it were an indisputable fact of life.

Sadly, any negative message you hear repeatedly in your younger years will quickly start to become factual for you and will be stored in what is known as your body's belief system. As with your mind, this belief system doesn't discern whether these messages are true or not (or even if they are yours or other people's!) — it simply stores the belief away for future use. As a result, your negative belief system also contains a significant amount of spam that you continue to believe to be true about yourself. Don't get me wrong, this is not an exercise in pointing the blame finger at people around you — remember, most of them are simply replaying the programming they soaked up when they were children, but it still doesn't mean that you have to believe any of it!

> **'Growing up I repeatedly heard that I was the "clever child" and my sister was the attractive one. As a result, although I excelled in my career, I have never felt good enough for a relationship, and the thought of flirting terrifies me. I just believe deep down that I am not attractive.' Alex, 29**

The beliefs we hold can be positive or negative, empowering or disempowering. They can be so deeply embedded inside us from such a young age, that we continue to view ourselves and the world according to them, even as an adult. These beliefs also determine what we think we are capable of, or not capable of. As a result, any negative programming we receive about ourselves can be particularly harmful when it relates to our sense of self, confidence and self-esteem.

Most of the time, we are not even aware of these negative beliefs, because they happen automatically at the subconscious level. It is fair to say that each of us will be programmed to hold negative beliefs that are as unique as the different families we grew up in. However, in my coaching experience I have found that there is a set of common, core negative beliefs that many of us hold. These include:

- **There is something wrong with me.**
- **I am not good enough.**
- **I am not wanted.**

- **I am not enough.**

- **I am not loveable.**

- **I am 'less than' or inferior to other people.**

- **I am bad.**

ANGELA

Angela grew up in a family of perfectionists and high achievers. As a result, the programming she received during her formative years included comments such as, 'You need to try harder.' Her family was only trying to help Angela strive to achieve good grades but unfortunately she decided that this meant that nothing she did was ever good enough and she always needed to do more in order to equal, or be accepted by, other people. As an adult, this led to Angela failing to put herself up for a promotion or speak up during meetings because she simply believed that however hard she tried, she would always fall short of other people's expectations. Interestingly, she was also an avid fan of the gym, often pushing herself to the state of exhaustion, believing that she always had to do better.

The good news is that we can easily reverse the effects of any negative programming, regardless of how many years we have spent believing it. I personally have overcome a wide range of negative beliefs including feeling not good enough, not worthy and also not believing I am loveable. Fortunately, I also freed myself from the belief that I was second best to every attractive woman on this planet! Therefore I urge you to not get discouraged by your own negative beliefs. We can learn to let them go as easily as we throw out the clothes that no longer fit us.

CHANGING THE PROGRAMMING

The first step in changing this old negative programming is to commit to finally letting go of these old ways of thinking. I will of course assist you with this but I require a personal commitment from you. Many people feel anxious about releasing old familiar programming because it may have become a comfortable and familiar part of their life. However, I promise that in choosing to let go of this negative programming, you will be giving your confidence muscle a well-deserved boost.

The first step is very important: you must try to see how flawed this entire programming and belief system really is. It may have served you well to receive some initial programming and influences that helped you develop as a child and keep you safe, but do you think it is still a good idea to live your life according to information you were programmed with decades ago?

If you picked up an old newspaper that was published when you were a child, would you still accept that everything featured in it is 100 per cent accurate? Of course not — things have changed, and so have you. You wouldn't fit into the clothes you wore as a child, so why would the old programming you are carrying around still fit you today?

The truth is, we can't change the past, but we can change and update our programming to reflect who we are today. You are no longer a child, and as an adult you can choose to let go of these outdated beliefs and replace them with new, updated beliefs — ones that support you and reflect not the child you were in the past, but the adult you want to become now.

ACTION STEP

Take a few minutes to look back over your childhood and recall any negative programming that you may have received from other people. Make a note of how this programming influences you now — this could relate to anything, such as your career, relationships, body image or perception of success. Look at your notes and simply acknowledge that as a child you had no control over this programming.

TOP TIPS FOR LETTING GO OF NEGATIVE PROGRAMMING

- Choose to fill your mind with new, updated programming that supports you as an adult.

- Choose to release yourself from any beliefs that do not serve you. Despite what you might have been taught to believe, the programming you received is not the truth — it is spam you have soaked up like a sponge from other people.

- Remember that most of the time the people who influence you with negative programming are not aware of the impact and damage it can have on your lifelong belief system.

- Regardless of any doubts you may have, remind yourself that you deserve to have confidence and you can do it!

- Remind yourself that there is nothing wrong with you; you are not fatally flawed in any way.

CHAPTER 4

WORRYING ABOUT WHAT OTHER PEOPLE THINK

So far, we have discussed the ways early negative programming can hold us back and block confidence, and we have also explored the importance of creating a new positive mindset.

Each and every one of us is unique, and therefore so are the raft of beliefs and fears that may have prevented us from living a confident life. One negative belief that I constantly come across with my clients, however, is the habit of always worrying about what other people think, or the fear of being judged by others. This fear can often raise its ugly head when we think about behaving in a more confident manner around other people — especially when it comes to being assertive or standing up for ourselves.

I think it is fair to say that as human beings, we tend to worry far too much about what people think of us, whether it is someone in our family, a new partner or even a complete stranger. We worry about our appearance, our intelligence and what others might think of the choices we have made in life. We might feel inferior to others and afraid that they will judge us negatively, or that they will think less of us if we do or say something wrong. Many of us censor what we really feel and go as far as amending what we say in front of other people just in case it doesn't please them. We fear disapproval, rejection or abandonment — we might even worry that those we care about will end up withdrawing their love from us.

TONY

CASE STUDY

Tony had worked in a large established accountancy firm for over ten years. He was successful and brought home a large salary that enabled him to live comfortably. However, in the past few years Tony had started to get bored and wished that he could leave his accountancy job and set up his own company assisting small-business owners to increase their sales revenue. Unfortunately, Tony came from a long line of people who believed that job security was more of a priority than job satisfaction. In fact, members of his family often told Tony how lucky he was to have a 'job for life' within a safe and secure profession. Tony feared the judgement and backlash from his family so much that, despite having a strong desire to set up his own business, he put his own needs aside and continued to work in his current role.

Worrying what people think of us leads to confidence-draining people-pleasing behaviour. A people-pleaser tries their hardest to keep everyone around them happy — often at their own expense. They may turn themselves inside out in order to please others, often doing things they really don't want to do. They usually end up saying yes when they really want to say no and will tell you that everything is fine even if they feel upset or, more often than not, feel taken advantage of or resentful. Many people-pleasers are expert peacekeepers and always want to be seen as a 'nice person', living their life according to other people's expectations, rather than their own.

This people-pleasing habit often stems from a deep belief that we need to look after other people's happiness and wellbeing at all costs and a deep fear of what may happen if we don't. Often, people with the 'disease to please' were brought up in families who avoided conflict and as a result, they picked up programming such as 'You shouldn't upset anyone,' or 'You must always be a nice person.' They may also have been raised in an environment where they felt it was their responsibility to keep family members happy. This is particularly prevalent where children are brought up in abusive families and may learn from a young age that in order to avoid conflict, it is safer for them to keep others happy.

> **'I was taught from a very early age to always "keep the peace" and never do anything to upset another person. I still avoid conflict as I just don't feel safe in speaking up in case someone disapproves of me or doesn't like what I have to say.' Emma, 54**

However, in truth, people-pleasing behaviour results in neglecting our own needs and wants. Ironically, a people-pleaser is often overlooked, taken for granted and loses the respect of the very people they are trying to please!

> **'I just couldn't bring myself to say no when my boss regularly asked me to stay late. I was worried that he would think that I wasn't committed enough.' Michelle, 29**

When I was younger, I suffered dreadfully from the 'disease to please', which as an adult unfortunately led me to stay in an unhealthy relationship for over four years. I would frequently go out of my way just to please my partner, even at a high cost to my emotional wellbeing. When I look back at this situation now, I can see how easily I gave my happiness and wellbeing away to another person. The truth was that I was more interested in keeping him happy than keeping myself happy, and I would have done anything to be seen in a positive light and to prevent conflict.

From experience I can tell you that giving up the 'disease to please' does not need to be difficult. It can be done — it just takes a little courage and practice. The good news is that when you start to release the attachment to pleasing everyone around you, you will begin to feel much safer within yourself and will find it less of a struggle to be authentic and confident. Start right now by working through the following action step and then reading the tips below.

ACTION STEP

Take the time to consider the questions below and write your thoughts in your journal:

- **Why you are trying so hard to be liked by everyone else? Do you really think it is possible for everyone to like you?**

- **In what situations and with whom do you find yourself displaying people-pleasing behaviour?**

- **How regularly do you stop yourself from doing or saying something, out of fear that someone won't like you or that you may offend them?**

TOP TIPS FOR RELEASING PEOPLE-PLEASING BEHAVIOURS

- If you recognize yourself as a people-pleaser, acknowledge that you can do something about it.

- If you worry about being judged, remind yourself that it is extremely likely that people are not even thinking about you. This is just your own mind creating this illusion.

- Try to keep things in context. People will always think what they want to think anyway — so, does it really matter in the big scheme of life?

- Learn to approve of yourself rather than always seeking approval from other people. What is more important: what others think of you or what you think about yourself?

- Take small steps to accommodate yourself, rather than always accommodating other people.

- Remember that you always have a choice to say 'no'. Just because someone asks for your help, you don't always have to say 'yes'. Look at saying 'no' and declining other people's requests as good self-care for you.

- Get clear on your own priorities in life. What is important to you? How do you wish to spend your time? Remember, you have the right to decide what to do, who to spend time with and to fulfil your own needs.

- Don't scare yourself worrying about other people's reactions. Just because you have said 'no' to someone, it doesn't mean the fallout will be terrible. Learn to soothe yourself through your fears and acknowledge that other people's reactions are rarely as bad as you think they might be.

WHAT DO YOU MAKE YOUR PERSONAL EXPERIENCES MEAN ABOUT YOU?

If someone doesn't like you or disapproves of you — how do you interpret this? What do you make it mean about you? If someone criticizes your life, or you believe that you may have upset them, what do you make it mean about you? If you experience rejection, what do you make it mean about you? Those who struggle with confidence are prone to attach negative meanings to life's experiences, usually seeing themselves in a poor light or blaming themselves for what is happening around them.

Let me give you an example of attaching a negative meaning to a relationship experience. Imagine you have been dating a new person for a while and they don't call you for a few days. How do you react to this? What do you make it mean about you? If you tend to attach a negative meaning, you may assume that the person is not interested in you, and allow your thoughts to snowball until you believe that you must have done something wrong or stupid, otherwise the person would have been in touch by now. You might immediately assume the worst has happened without having any factual evidence to back it up.

'If I get turned down for a job, I immediately make this mean that there is something wrong with me or that I am not intelligent or good enough.' Emma, 34

JENNY

Jenny always worried that people didn't like her. She used to go out of her way to please other people and keep them happy. One Saturday evening, Jenny held a dinner party for ten of her friends but two of them left her a message a short time before the party started, stating they were unable to attend. As a result, Jenny couldn't relax to enjoy the

evening as she worried about what she might have done to cause her friends to cancel.

In the above case study, can you see how Jenny had decided to make it mean something negative about her that her friends had not come to her party? In her mind she had already decided that she was at fault, and that somehow she was the reason for her friends not showing up.

At this stage Jenny actually had no idea why her friends hadn't showed up but she automatically jumped to a negative conclusion, blaming herself. A few days later, Jenny discovered the facts when she received a phone call from her friends explaining that the reason they hadn't turned up was due to a family emergency.

If we struggle with self-confidence, we can become masterful at jumping to conclusions, blaming ourselves and taking things personally if things don't go according to plan. It is far healthier, however, to our sense of self and confidence if we begin to attach positive assumptions and facts to our experiences, rather than automatically jumping to negative meanings and conclusions.

If we reflect back on our earlier relationship example — in which you were dating someone new and they hadn't contacted you for a few days — we can see a clear way of changing the negative into a positive. Rather than making this event mean something negative — and trying to read minds — it would be much healthier to stick to the black-and-white facts of why the person hadn't called you. Remember, all the negative assumptions you make are simply figments of your imagination, and at this stage you don't have any other factual evidence to support your theory that the person is no longer interested. Have you considered that they may just be busy? Or that maybe they thought that they shouldn't appear too keen? Even if the 'worst' did happen and you never heard from them again, a far better interpretation would be to accept that it simply didn't work out, put it down to experience and move on to find someone with whom you are more compatible. Wouldn't that feel much nicer? And wouldn't this actually be more sensible and real?

Whatever happens to us, whatever experiences we may be part of, we have a choice whether to interpret them as positive or negative. This technique does take a little practice at first but have patience with yourself. It is particularly beneficial when you find yourself fearing the worst, without exploring the actual facts of the situation.

ACTION STEP

Take a few minutes to reflect on the following questions and make any notes in your journal:

- **If you believe that someone doesn't like you, what do you make that mean about you?**

- **If someone doesn't agree with what you are doing, what do you make that mean about you?**

- **If someone criticizes you, what do you make that mean about you?**

- **If someone does not approve of you, what do you make that mean about you?**

- **If someone rejects you, what do you make that mean about you?**

Remember, you do always have a choice to either assume the negative or assume the positive. When you do practise assuming the positive, not only will you attract all sorts of new opportunities, you will also start to improve your self-image.

TOP TIPS FOR POSITIVE INTERPRETATIONS

- **Don't jump to conclusions too quickly.**

- **Create positive interpretations rather than automatic negative assumptions.**

- **Don't fall into the trap of believing everything you think!**

- **Challenge your thoughts — are they based on factual information or just speculation?**

CHAPTER 5

LEARNING TO VALUE YOURSELF

Learning to acknowledge yourself as a valuable human being is a key foundation for self-confidence. Unfortunately, many of us were not taught at an early age to place sufficient value on ourselves, and as a result we place too little importance on our own needs, wants and desires.

If you feel that what other people want is more important than what *you* want, then you are failing to value yourself. If you believe that other people's happiness is more important than your own happiness, then you are failing to value yourself. Think about it — if you don't value yourself, why should anyone else?

Valuing yourself is about recognizing that you have equal value to everyone else on this planet and have the right to look after yourself and ask for what you want. It is about recognizing and respecting your own needs and wants, and treating yourself with respect. You have the right to choose to do what is right for you rather than always doing what other people want you to do. Valuing yourself comes from trusting your own judgement and from living by your own personal expectations rather than the expectations of other people.

MELINDA

CASE STUDY

Melinda enjoyed nothing more than relaxing at home on a Saturday night reading a book. However, her best friend Cherie preferred to spend the weekends in the local bars, usually finishing her Saturday night in a nightclub.

Every Saturday morning, Melinda would receive a call from Cherie, pleading with her to join her in the evening for a big night out. Although Melinda was tired and just fancied a quiet night in, her inner voice told her it would be selfish and that Cherie may get upset if she said no. As a result, Melinda spent most of her precious Saturday nights in a bar, wishing that she was back at home, relaxing, curled up with her favourite book. As this went on for several months, Melinda started to feel resentful towards her friend and began to make up all types of excuses just to avoid her calls.

In this example, can you see how Melinda didn't value herself or her time? She believed that what Cherie wanted was far more important than what *she* wanted. In fact, she disregarded her own needs just to avoid upsetting her friend.

In a nutshell, Melinda valued Cherie's needs far more than she valued her own.

Are you one of those people who say 'yes' when you really mean 'no'? Do you end up choosing the smallest portion of cake so that other people can have the biggest slice? Do you agree to do something and then feel resentful for it afterwards? If so, then it is time to start valuing yourself and taking care of your own needs, rather than neglecting them in order to look after other people. When you start to feel resentful it is usually a sign that you have placed more importance on someone else's needs than on your own. Remember, as human beings we all have equal value, worth and dignity. Taking care of your needs is not selfishness; it is an act of self-care.

In the following chapter, we look at a key technique to assist you in acknowledging your own value and paying attention to your own needs.

YOUR PERSONAL BILL OF RIGHTS

One of the neat little tricks that I use to remind myself of the importance of valuing myself and taking care of my own needs is to write down my 'Personal Bill of Rights'. (I first came across this idea through the work of Edmund Bourne, PhD, in his book *The Anxiety and Phobia Workbook*.) This is a great reminder to myself that I deserve to be a priority in my own life and that I do have the same human rights as everyone else on this planet. Below I have highlighted my own Personal Bill of Rights. These rights are not just unique to me, they are applicable to you, and every other person living and breathing on this planet.

My Personal Bill of Rights

- **I have the right to choose how and when to fulfil my own needs, even if my choices conflict with other people's opinions or desires.**

- **I have the right to my own personal time and to choose what I want to do with it.**

- **I have the right to make myself and my choices my first priority.**

- **I have the right to do what makes me feel happy, even if it does not make other people happy.**

- **I have the right to care for and look after my own needs.**

- **I have the right to set my own rules and priorities.**

- **I have the right to say what I feel.**

- **I have the right to express my opinions and beliefs.**

- **I have the right to change my mind if I feel like it.**

- **I have the right not to make a decision until I am ready to do so.**

- **I have the right to say 'yes' or 'no' without having to explain myself.**

- **I have the right to decline responsibility for other people's problems.**

- **I have the right to be illogical in making decisions.**

- **I have the right to be listened to, and taken seriously.**

- **I have the right to make mistakes.**

- **I have the right to choose my friends and acquaintances and decide when to spend time with them. I do not have to justify these choices to others.**

- **I have the right to respectfully tell others how their actions are affecting me.**

When you read over the list, were any of the rights surprising to you? Did you realize you had all of these human rights? Learning to exercise these rights will help you build up your confidence muscle and become a more assertive person, and through this book I will help you to do this.

ACTION STEP

- In your journal, write a list of your own personal needs and wants. What is important to you?

- Design your own Personal Bill of Rights and display it somewhere where it will act as a regular reminder that your opinions and needs are just as important as everyone else's.

TOP TIPS FOR VALUING YOURSELF

- Refer to your Personal Bill of Rights regularly, particularly if you feel used, discounted or disrespected by other people.

- Prioritize your own needs.

- Notice when you start to feel resentful. This is a clear sign that you are failing to value yourself and your own needs.

- Set yourself a target to say 'no' (when you would normally say 'yes') at least once a week.

- Just because someone has asked you to do something, it doesn't mean you have to agree.

CHAPTER 6

FEELING SAFE TO MAKE CHANGES

When we begin to release old programming and beliefs and start to practise new healthy habits, we may feel apprehensive, frightened or unsafe. Many of us fear giving up old patterns or familiar ways of behaviour such as people-pleasing. This is partly due to the fear of the unknown, which makes us feel anxious and scared. This reaction can be particularly common for people who in the past have experienced negative consequences for failing to do what other people expected them to do. As a result, they learn from an early age to keep other people happy in order to avoid losing that all-important love or approval. Sadly, many people have experienced physical or emotional abuse if they didn't keep the people around them happy.

It doesn't feel good to have a fearful mind. It not only makes us feel helpless and trapped but it keeps us small, stuck in old ways and familiar outcomes. Ultimately, a fearful mind stops us from stepping into our greatness and creates a never-ending cycle of even more fearful experiences. In addition, a mind that is filled with fear creates a tired and exhausted body due to the constant struggle with our own thoughts.

Our mind plays an important role in reminding us to be cautious, particularly in matters of life and death. However, sometimes it holds tightly to past outcomes in our life, fooling us into believing that something is more frightening than it really is or making fearful assumptions that history will repeat itself.

ROSIE

CASE STUDY

Several years ago Rosie joined a running club and was keen to make new friends. She invited one of the girls round to dinner and when the girl declined her offer without explanation, Rosie felt embarrassed and rejected.

Rosie still attends the running club several times a month, but she tends to run alone and avoids socializing with the other members. As soon as each session ends she usually jumps straight into her car to go home, as her mind has full control over her, convincing her that it isn't safe to speak to the other members just in case she ends up feeling embarrassed or rejected again. Unfortunately, Rosie chose to listen to these scary thoughts, rather than creating her own mindset of safety.

Remember we talked about the confidence muscle in the earlier chapters in this book? An important step in growing this muscle is being able to build a feeling of safety within your own mind, regardless of what other people are saying and doing around you. Feeling emotionally safe means that you trust your ability to cope, even if other people don't like it.

You may have felt scared as a child, but now as an adult you can choose to take personal responsibility for creating your own mindset of safety using your own inner dialogue and self-talk. This in turn will reduce your fears and make it more comfortable for you to introduce new confident behaviours.

I am not suggesting you should ever stay around people who are abusive or threaten to harm you. However, there are circumstances in which many of us are still unconsciously running on old fearful programming in our minds that can be far more frightening than the reality of the situation we are faced with.

Most of us also fear standing up for ourselves or being more assertive because we believe that it will lead to some type of conflict. As a result, we try to avoid these circumstances at all costs — choosing to take the 'easier' passive- or avoidance route. It is at these very times that our mind can take over with a flood of fearful unsafe thoughts such as:

- **I know they're not going to like it; what if they get angry?**
- **What if something bad happens or things go wrong?**
- **It's safer for me not to do anything.**
- **I will only feel guilty, so I won't bother.**
- **It's not worth it; I'll just keep quiet.**

These fearful thoughts can impact our professional and personal lives, keeping us stuck in old behaviours as we fear the consequences of our new actions.

> **'Deep down, I knew exactly what changes I needed to make in my life, but whenever it became time to actually implement the changes, my thoughts would spiral into fears of how people may react towards me and what could go wrong. This led to me feeling stuck in the same old situations for many years because I was too scared to take action.' Kirstie, 32**

NORA

Nora's partner Joe was a bit of a flirt, and when they went out with friends he would often pay more attention to Nora's friends than to her. When they were alone, though, he was kind and attentive to Nora. Rather than speaking to Joe and explaining how she felt and asking him to change his behaviour, Nora listened to the thoughts in her head that told her it would be safer to keep quiet and say nothing, just in case Joe got upset or it caused an argument between them. As a result, nothing changed and Nora started to feel increasingly resentful towards Joe. She even stopped catching up with her friends because she didn't want to feel upset if Joe continued his usual behaviour.

Let's look at this a little more objectively and begin to fill our mind with a few thoughts that will help create a mindset of safety.

Have you ever considered that it is perfectly normal for someone not to like everything you say or do, and to occasionally disagree with you? Have you thought that despite your fears, you could in fact cope with it? Have you realized that as an adult you can choose to walk away from someone if you don't feel comfortable? Have you also considered that this may be your mind playing tricks on you, assuming that the worst would happen — when in reality everything could work out fine and most people are actually quite reasonable? (We will deal with bullies in a later chapter.) Why do you assume that you wouldn't be able to handle it?

This is when it is so important to remind yourself that you can trust yourself and you will be okay — remember, you are capable of coping! So what if someone doesn't approve of what you are doing? Do you need to attach a negative meaning to this or can you just accept that we are all different and let it go? Are you going to put more faith in their opinion of you than your own? Why is their opinion so important to you? Do they know you better than you know you? So what if someone doesn't like you? Are they important in your life anyway? Do you even care that they don't like you? Why do you value what *they* think rather than valuing what *you* think?

When one of my clients is feeling scared of upsetting someone, I simply ask them: what is the worst that could happen? Be really honest with yourself: would you die if this person didn't like you? Would you fall apart and lose everything? Of course you wouldn't! In reality, it is only our own thoughts that can frighten us, making things seem worse than they are and causing us to doubt ourselves.

Feeling unsafe also stems from a lack of trust or faith in yourself that you can cope. This is very important, so let's look again at this in more detail.

Trusting yourself plays a huge part in whether you feel safe to make changes. Self-confident people trust their own abilities — they know they can cope. By this I mean that they believe, within reason, that they can handle whatever life throws at them, even if they are judged negatively or people don't like or approve of them. It doesn't mean they know they will do everything perfectly, but they do trust in their ability to work things out. They know that they will be okay. As a result, they don't put so much energy or focus into worrying about the disapproval of others.

CASE STUDY

THOMAS

Thomas had recently lent his close friend a small sum of money, which had not been repaid. Prior to working on his confidence, Thomas would easily have bought into the scary thoughts in his head that told him that it was not safe to ask for his money back, in case he annoyed or upset his friend. However, armed with a stronger confidence muscle, Thomas realized

that in order to value himself and take care of his own needs he needed to be assertive and request that the money be repaid. He reminded himself that even if his friend did get annoyed, he would be able to handle it. Therefore, Thomas bit the bullet and simply called his friend and asked that he pay him back. His friend had simply forgotten and paid Thomas back the money that very day.

This case study shows that in order for you to expand that confidence muscle a little bit more, it is important to put some effort into making yourself feel safe and putting greater trust in yourself. This includes knowing deep down that you have an infinite right to speak up, make mistakes, embarrass yourself, say no, ask for a pay rise, leave work early — and still feel like a great person on the inside regardless of whether or not other people approve of you.

Take a few minutes to think about the children in your life. They could be your own, a family member's children or just simply children you know. (If you are struggling to think of one, you can even think of a pet or an animal you love.)

I want you to imagine that this child or animal you love is feeling scared and anxious because they are going to try something new for the very first time.

Now ask yourself: what words would they most like to hear? What would you say to them that might soothe their fears about trying something new? Would you hold the child or pet and give it a huge hug reminding it that it doesn't need to be afraid? Would you tell them that everything is going to be okay and that they are safe? Would you tell them that whatever they are attempting might feel a little scary at first but then they will simply get used to it and may even enjoy it?

The fact is, most of us try too hard to remove fears before we do anything, and this is not the easiest way. You need to start by encouraging yourself and telling yourself that you are capable and you will be okay. Going forward, I would love you to remember the encouraging and soothing words you would share with this child or pet and use them on yourself whenever you feel scared. This will really start to build up your mindset of safety.

Here are a few ideas for creating a safety mindset. Repeat them to yourself whenever you feel you need that extra bit of encouragement.

- **I know that I feel scared about speaking up and saying 'no', but I am going to be okay — I am capable and hey, what is the worst that can happen?**

- **I know I don't like saying 'no' to my mum but in time it will get easier. The good thing is that I am learning to take care of myself and feel more confident. Okay, she may not like it but I can cope. I will be okay.**

- **I feel nervous about asking my friend for the money she owes me. However, what is the worst that could happen? Even if she doesn't like it, I know that I will feel better for asking her, because I am starting to feel resentful towards her. I can do this, even though I feel afraid. I am valuing myself by asking for what I would like to happen.**

ACTION STEP

Think about some of the things you fear happening. Is it that someone won't like you or you may upset someone? Write down your thoughts, and then ask yourself: what is really the worst that could happen?

TOP TIPS FOR FEELING SAFE

- Assume things will go well, rather than making frightening assumptions.

- Create safety in your mind by using words and phrases that soothe your fears and encourage you to step out of your comfort zone.

- Don't allow the fears of how other people may react to you hold you back from speaking up and asking for what you want.

- If you always feel scared about speaking up around certain people, it could be time to remove them from your life. This is often a good thing!

- Trust yourself that things will work out for the best.

CHAPTER 7

FEELING UNCOMFORTABLE

W henever we start to let go of old behaviours and implement new thought patterns and actions, whether it is learning to be assertive, asking for what we want or putting plans in place to look after our own needs, we are always going to go through a period of feeling emotionally uncomfortable. This uncomfortable feeling may arrive in your body shortly after you have spoken up, plucked up the courage to say 'no' to another person or simply chosen to do what works or feels right for you, rather than what another person expects you to do.

It is important to be aware of this uncomfortable feeling, because it can trip you up, fooling you into believing that it is an indicator that you have done something wrong. Be careful not to pay too much attention to it, because it will keep you stuck in old negative behaviours and prevent you from being the confident person you want to be.

This uncomfortable feeling — whether it fills you with guilt or anxiety, or causes you to label yourself a bad person or simply feel deep down that you have done something wrong — is a perfectly normal reaction to change. Look at it this way; you are building up your confidence muscle, so it is bound to feel a bit different from what you are used to. In actual fact, this uncomfortable emotion is actually a good indicator that you are changing into a more confident person and healthy change is in progress.

> **'I finally stood up to my mum, informing her that I would no longer be able to come round to see her every day. It felt great for a few days … until I started to feel guilty and beat myself up. As a result, I just went back to my old ways of running around after her on a daily basis because it just felt easier.' Nicole, 42**

Remember, at first you will feel different, and a bit uncomfortable, as you change old habits and programming you may have had for a lifetime. Remind yourself that this feeling is just like any other emotion, giving you an indication of how you are feeling at one moment in time. What makes this emotion so darn tricky is that the majority of us tend to see it as a sign that something is wrong and that we need to do something to fix it. We may use it as an excuse to beat ourselves up and doubt our decisions or actions, and this in turn may make us feel that it is easier to release this feeling by going back to old and more comfortable and familiar ways of behaviour.

PETER

Peter was a family man with a wife and two small children. He worked for a large organization and all his co-workers were happy to work twelve to fifteen hours a day, often staying in the office until late in the evening. Peter recognized that he also often stayed late — not because he had lots of work to do, but he felt that if he left the office on time, people would talk about him behind his back or think he was lazy. For his own happiness and wellbeing, Peter decided he wanted to spend more time with his family, and committed to leave the office by 5.30pm two days a week. He felt happy to do this, and despite the anxiety and fears that played in his mind, he packed up his stuff and left the office on time. As a result, Peter spent a lovely few hours at home with his family and felt great that he had taken action.

However, several hours into the evening he started to feel uncomfortable and his mindset changed to, 'What if my boss thinks I am not up to the job? What if people are judging me and talking about me behind my back?'

Fortunately, Peter recognized this uncomfortable feeling as what it simply was — an indicator that he was doing things differently and changing old programming. Peter soothed himself with kind words, repeating that things were going to be okay. He knew that it was important to create a safe mindset in his head and he continued to remind himself that change was going to feel a little different and uncomfortable for a while. He reminded himself that he was valuing himself and his family and this was an important step for him to take. Going forward, it gradually became easier for Peter to leave work on time and he became a far happier person now that he was looking after his own needs.

Had Peter given in to the uncomfortable feeling, he may have ended up going back to the old pattern of working all those long hours every day — all the while feeling resentful and wishing that he could change.

Guilt can also lead us to feel uncomfortable. Most of us feel guilty at some point in our lives. Healthy guilt is an emotional indicator that we have acted against our own values or convictions. However, unhealthy guilt may raise its ugly head after we step into a new confident behaviour, eating away at our good intentions and positive mindset. Too many of us see guilt as a reason to keep ourselves stuck, make amends or go back to our people-pleasing behaviours.

JULIE

Julie was always looking after other people. She would run herself into the ground, doing other people's shopping, picking up their kids, and generally agreeing to do anything that people asked of her. She came to me looking for assistance in building up her confidence muscle because she realized that although she didn't mind occasionally helping people, she was starting to feel resentful that people never seemed to reciprocate her kindness and at times she felt they took advantage of her because they presumed that, as a single woman, she had a lot of spare time.

After doing some coaching work with Julie, I discovered that one of her core negative beliefs was that she should never upset anyone. Even the mere thought of speaking up and saying 'no' filled Julie with fear — she believed that it could end in conflict or that someone would get upset with her. It was no surprise that as a result of this programming Julie had spent most of her life running around after other people trying to keep them happy!

Julie decided that it was time to take control and build up her confidence muscle. She resolved that her first step would be to inform her friend that she could no longer look after her kids each and every Saturday morning when her friend went to the gym. Julie had been helping her friend out for several months but it was leaving her tired and exhausted, with little time to herself over the weekend.

Importantly, Julie first worked on her mindset, re-affirming with encouraging words that she could do this and that everything was going to be okay. She also reminded herself that the worst thing that could happen was that her friend would be annoyed or perhaps would not speak to her again. After acknowledging this, Julie realized that this would be okay because she often felt that this person was not really a good friend anyway and often took advantage of Julie's kind nature. Although of course she still felt anxious about speaking up to her friend, Julie encouraged herself to go ahead, soothed her fears and reminded herself that it was always a good idea to value her own needs and wants.

The result was that Julie's friend was not happy! She got rather upset and told Julie that she felt let down. They ended up having an argument and Julie went home feeling guilty and uncomfortable.

Julie was tempted to ring her friend back, apologize and agree to look after the kids the following Saturday, but she remembered that the uncomfortable emotion that she was feeling was just part of growing her confidence muscle — and she also reminded herself of how much she was looking forward to having Saturday mornings all to herself. A few old negative thoughts filled Julie's mind, telling her that she was selfish and a bad person for upsetting her friend, but again Julie recognized these thoughts as old programming and was able to calm her thoughts by replacing them with words of encouragement and support. As a result, she decided to watch some TV and take care of herself instead.

Two days later, Julie's friend called her to apologize for her behaviour. She told Julie she totally understood and was sorry for taking advantage of her in the past. As a result, they have a great friendship and Julie no longer feels resentful — in fact, she feels confident and empowered.

The feeling of discomfort is an indicator that can either propel you forward into confidence, or keep you stuck in old behaviour patterns.

Choose to interpret it as a sign that you are moving away from old pro-gramming and into new-found confidence! If this uncomfortable feeling grows particularly strong within you, please work through it as best as you can.

TOP TIPS TO WORK THROUGH THE UNCOMFORTABLE FEELING

- **Recognize that this is a normal feeling — it is nothing to fear.**

- **Learn to soothe yourself with a simple statement such as, 'I know it may not feel like it right now, but everything is working out okay for me.'**

- **Look at the uncomfortable feeling with a positive mindset; the truth is it means that you are doing a detox of old familiar patterns and building up your confidence.**

- **If the uncomfortable feeling gets really strong, go for a walk or pick up the phone and chat to someone who will encourage you through it until the feeling passes.**

CHAPTER 8

TAKING BACK YOUR POWER

Let's now introduce the concept of personal power. This may come as a surprise to you (it certainly did to me when I first discovered it!) but everyone on this planet was born with personal power. This power gives each and every one of us the freedom of choice. It allows us, among other things, to choose what we wear, what food we like to eat, whom we wish to hang out with, what job we take and how we communicate with other people. Put simply, this personal power gives us the choice of how we want to live our life. When we choose to use this power constructively it supplies us with the freedom to firmly take up the reins of our own life and to do the things that are important to us and make us happy.

When you own and work with your personal power, you also have a choice about how you treat people and how you allow other people to treat you. You have the freedom to choose to accept poor behaviour from others or to put a stop to it. You have a choice to moan about your job or to take action and do something positive about it. You have a choice to let other people tell you what to do or to decide what you personally want to do.

To put it simply, you have a choice to be a victim of life or to take responsibility for your life and the choices that come with it. The truth is that people can only take away our personal power if we give it to them.

Many of us, consciously or unconsciously, give our power away to other people. Instead of taking responsibility for our life and recognizing that we always have a choice, we keep ourselves stuck by blaming other people or situations for the way we feel or how our lives have turned out. We also render ourselves as victims of circumstances, choosing to blame other people for upsetting us or hurting us in some way. Many of us blame our children or parents or other people in our lives for causing us stress or preventing us from doing what we really want to do.

Other ways you might give away your power include:

- **Allowing other people to dump the 'guilt trip' on you.**
- **Taking responsibility for other people's problems.**
- **Going against your own best interests.**
- **Allowing other people to control, manipulate or abuse you.**
- **Complaining about things but doing nothing to change them.**
- **Always blaming other people for what is happening in your life.**

People who choose to give away their power will often use statements such as:

- **'It is my parents' fault that I have no confidence.'**

- **'If only my boss would change, everything would be okay.'**

- **'I can't go out for a night out; my partner wouldn't like it.'**

- **'If only I could lose more weight, I would feel much happier.'**

At any given time you have a choice about how you react to, or feel about any situation. You can choose to point the finger of blame at other people and feel resentful, or you can choose to take back your personal power and take responsibility for your own life and your own choices. For example, you can continue to blame your parents for the programming you received as a child or you can choose to take responsibility and do something positive about it.

Every time you allow negative feelings, fears or other people's opinions to block you from moving forward, you are also choosing to give your power away. When you allow other people to upset you, control you or put you down, you have chosen to give your power away. Each time you care too much about what others think and give in to what other people want for you rather than what *you* want, you have given away your personal power. Many of us continue through adulthood to give our power away to old beliefs and programming, rendering ourselves as victims of our own past.

The truth about personal power is that we choose to give it away — people cannot take it from us without our permission. We have a choice to improve any situation we are in. True personal power comes from recognizing your personal value and self-worth and knowing that you always have a choice. When you choose to own your power, you give yourself the permission to do what you want to do and take responsibility for your own life, happiness and wellbeing, regardless of other people's opinions and judgements.

I like to think that personal power is like a big bus adventure: you can choose to sit in the driver's seat of your life, going to the places that make you happy, doing the things that give you joy and generally driving your own life bus in the direction you want your life to go — or you can choose to give your power or driver's seat over to another person, allowing them to influence how you behave, where you go and ultimately, how happy you are.

MARY

Ever since Mary was a small child, her mum had been very critical of her, particularly about her appearance and weight. As an adult, her mum continued to make regular critical comments towards her and after visiting her mum, Mary often felt upset and resentful, but she never felt she could do anything about it, so the pattern continued.

To whom has Mary given her power? Her mum! Rather than choosing to speak up about the hurtful comments from her mother, Mary has chosen to hand her power over, rendering herself powerless. As a result, it is Mary who ends up feeling upset and her mother really has no idea of the hurt she has caused.

I know that it may seem easier for Mary just to wish that her mother would change, but unfortunately we can't change other people. If you are sitting around waiting for something to change in order for you to feel better, you have given your power away to someone else — and you may have a long wait.

The fact is that Mary's mother may never change her behaviour. So, rather than wishing for her mother to change, Mary could make a conscious decision to choose to take back her power. There are various ways she could do this including:

- **Being assertive and speaking to her mother about how this behaviour is affecting her.**

- **Requesting that her mother stop her critical attitude.**

- **Putting some distance between herself and her mother for a while.**

- **Ignoring her mother's comments.**

- **Choosing not to allow the critical comments to upset her so much.**

- **Working on her own self-confidence so that her mother's comments do not bother her any more.**

Can you see that there is always a choice, and any of the above options would mean that Mary is choosing to take responsibility for her own life and take back her power from her mum?

Think about your life as it currently stands: are you driving your own bus or are you sitting in the back seat allowing other people to take control of your bus? To what or whom have you given your power? What are you going to do: are you going to continue to feel powerless or are you going to make a choice to do something about it? Owning your own personal power is about recognizing that nothing can actually control or influence you unless you allow it to.

There are many different ways you can start taking back your own personal power. First of all, notice how regularly you relinquish your power and recognize that most of the time it really doesn't feel good in your body either. In times when I feel I have given away my power, I just usually ask myself, 'What three things do I need to do right now that will allow me to take back my power?' These are often not huge actions, just little mindset changes or small steps that I need to take to reclaim my power.

Another great way to reclaim your personal power in your life is to begin to take a few seconds' breathing space before reacting or agreeing to do something. In these few seconds, you can stop and simply ask yourself the following questions:

- **Am I choosing to give my power away at this moment, and am I about to do something that is not in my best interest?**

- **Am I doing what I want to do due to my own choice or am I doing what other people want me to do?**

- **What needs to happen right now for me to reclaim my power in this situation?**

ACTION STEP

Take a few minutes to write the answers to the following questions in your journal:

- **Who or what in your life do you give your power away to?**

- **What are three things you can do to take back your power from somebody or a situation you find yourself in?**

TOP TIPS FOR PERSONAL POWER

- **Don't allow other people to have an unhealthy level of influence and control in your life.**

- **Remind yourself that getting angry and resentful at someone else will not change a thing.**

- **Recognize that if someone is critical towards you, you don't have to believe what they say or take it on board.**

- **Believe that a situation will change, when you change.**

CHAPTER 9

BUSTING THOSE EXCUSES

We are nearly at the end of Part One, in which we have started to shake up your negative programming and belief system. Going forward, we are going to continue to strengthen your confidence muscle and also focus on specific occasions in your life where you may need extra help, such as when you are dealing with a bully or feeling needy in a relationship.

Before we do, I want to bust any final excuses your mind may have started to create about continuing on this confidence journey. As I mentioned before, the human mind is complex, and there are a million reasons or excuses it can create to make you put down this book and give up on yourself.

These excuses may include the following sentiments:

- **It sounds too difficult; I won't be able to do it.**

- **There's no point, I've had this issue for years and there's nothing I can do to change it.**

- **I prefer not to rock the boat. It's just easier if I stay where I am now and don't make any changes.**

- **I'm too scared to change.**

- **Is it worth it — what if I disappoint myself again?**

- **I'm sure other people can do it, but I'm not sure I can.**

If any of these excuses is coming up for you, please don't allow it to make you give up or keep you from progressing any further. Bust these excuses and don't buy into them!

If you have been struggling with confidence for a while, it is perfectly normal to feel apprehensive about making changes. Remember, if you are feeling a little uncomfortable, this is a good thing. Keep control of your mindset and remind yourself that any excuses you may come up with right now are just positive indicators that changes are actually taking place. Don't allow your mind to trick you into thinking that you can't do it or things won't change. You *can* do it and I have faith in you!

CLAIRE

CASE STUDY

Claire was sick of not feeling confident at work. I set her some action steps to release some of her old programming, and she returned two weeks later complaining that nothing had changed and she had been too busy to work on her action steps.

Although Claire said she was committed to becoming more confident, can you see how she was coming up with all sorts of excuses to do nothing at all and stay in her comfort zone? The fact is that Claire's excuses were keeping her stuck.

Thankfully, after a quick pep talk with me, Claire decided to take back her power because she realized that she was the only person who could change her situation. The success or failure of her life was 100 per cent her own personal choice. As a result, Claire decided to bust her own excuses, and she knew deep down that she really did want to become a more confident person. As a result, Claire went on to complete her action steps and now has a strong confidence muscle and loves the effect this newfound confidence is having in her life.

If you decide that this is all too hard, when will you make the change? Five years? Ten years? Remember, nobody is coming to save you. If you want to feel more confident and your life to improve, you need to take responsibility and do something different from what you have always done.

Before we move on any further, take the time to reinforce these messages and re-program your mind with the following confidence reminders:

- **Give up the need to please other people and accept that many people are simply 'unpleasable' and there is nothing you can do to make them happy.**

- **Make a decision that your happiness is important to you. Change your focus from keeping other people happy and move towards making yourself happy.**

- **Change your mindset and remember that whenever you do something different, it is going to feel slightly uncomfortable. Remind yourself that you can cope and you will be okay. You are putting positive steps in place to build up your confidence and also feel better about yourself.**

- **Acknowledge that you have no control over how people**

react to you. However, you do have total control over how you choose to react. Simply put, you can allow other people's reactions to cause you to feel unsafe, or you can choose to feel safe whatever outcome or reaction you receive from other people.

- **Learn to disengage from other people's drama. The more importance you place on other people's reactions to you, the less safe you will feel. Try not to take things personally.**

- **Choose to take responsibility for your own life and reclaim your power.**

- **Choose to soothe and encourage yourself with kind words rather than allowing old negative programming to hijack your mind.**

The aim of Part One was to loosen up and clear away old programming and habitual destructive self-talk. In doing this, we have created space in our mind for new behaviour patterns to grow, which will lead to new ways of living. In the next section we will learn how to create the confident future we desire.

PART TWO

A Confident Future

CHAPTER 10

CONFIDENCE GOALS

Now that you have made a good start on clearing out some of your old baggage and negative programming, your journey into your new confident future will be much easier. Just by completing the action steps in the previous chapters you have already enabled your confidence muscle to grow on a firm foundation — rather than one that is shaky and filled with false premises and old negative programming. This groundwork will help you create the new confident habits I outline in the coming chapters.

We are going to start by setting some confidence goals.

I am sure many of you are familiar with goal-setting but just in case, here are some of the reasons why goal-setting for confidence is a great idea:

- **It helps you get excited about achieving confidence.**
- **It gives you an objective to work towards.**

- **Reading a goal regularly helps to instil new thought patterns and beliefs in your mind, thus creating a more positive mindset.**

- **It will inspire you into action and keep you accountable.**

- **It helps you think about what you do want, rather than what you don't want.**

Setting a confidence goal will help you create a clear vision of what being a confident person means to you; an outcome of how you want to look and feel once you become a more confident person. Take a few minutes now to think about the following:

- **What is your life going to look like when you have a strong confidence muscle?**

- **What will you be doing?**

- **How differently will you interact with people?**

- **How will it change your life for the better?**

- **Will you look different?**

- **How is it going to feel?**

> **'I just wanted to walk into a crowded room without feeling anxious or worrying that I was being judged by other people.' Shelly, 47**

Each and every one of us will have our own unique idea of how we want our life to be when we are masters of confidence. Therefore, choose to write a goal in whatever area of your life resonates with you. It could be a specific area such as confidence in relationships or career, or maybe a goal about feeling more confident in general. You can even just pick a specific situation that you feel you want to conquer, such as learning to say 'no' to a family member.

> **'I really wanted to be able to speak to my manager about the issues I was experiencing in the office.' Peter, 23**

The most important part of writing a confidence goal is that it should feel good to you. Okay, you may not believe that you can achieve it right now but the goal should make you want it and be excited about achieving it!

Let's face it, if you write a goal that you think is boring or looks difficult to achieve, it won't take long before you lose interest in it and easily fall back into old habits and behaviours. This is the main reason why many New Year's resolutions fail to work — they are more focused on giving up something (such as weight or chocolate) rather than achieving something that you really want. Many books on goal-setting also recommend that you write a goal as if you already have it and you are already the super-confident person you desire to be. In my experience, I have found that this often causes people to worry about how they are going to achieve the goal and they often get too bogged down in the detail. Therefore, when you write your goal, make sure it doesn't leave you feeling worried or disheartened — keep it simple, and ensure that it feels good when you read it.

GUIDELINES FOR WRITING A CONFIDENCE GOAL
STEP ONE — planning your confidence goal
Before you begin to write your confidence goals, it often helps to take a few minutes to remind yourself how your current lack of confidence in life may be holding you back. For example, is it preventing you from being assertive or asking for what you want? Does your low self-confidence stop you from taking risks or embarking on that career you have

always dreamed of? Does a lack of confidence have you constantly worried about other people's opinion of you?

Don't hold back from doing this — this process will often result in you feeling relief just by writing the answers down on paper and getting them out of your head.

Here is an example of step one:

- **I feel nervous when asking for what I want.**

- **I worry about what people will think of me.**

- **Even when I do find the courage to speak up, I end up feeling guilty.**

- **I feel I have to always do what other people want me to do.**

- **I always feel awkward in groups and think I have nothing interesting to say.**

STEP TWO — writing your confidence goal

Now it is time to construct your personal confidence goal. I have found that one of the easiest ways to do this is to look back at what you have written in Step One, and turn these situations on their head to focus on what you really want. Please don't get too tied up in the detail of the goal-setting process, just have some fun with it and write down how you would really like your life to be, as a confident person. There is simply no right or wrong way to write a goal — it just needs to feel right for you and you alone. Just make it feel good and exciting!

Here is an example of step two:
I am really looking forward to feeling more confident and being able to speak up comfortably without feeling nervous or guilty. I know it may feel scary right now but

I know I can do it and it is going to feel really good. I am learning how to feel safe and I know how good it is going to feel when I feel confident in making my own choices in my life and not worrying about what people will think.

The key test for your goal is to check in with yourself as you read it — does it feel good to you? Do you feel excited about achieving it? Always aim for the goal to feel easy and fun rather than a goal that sounds hard to achieve.

Never use this process as a reason to confuse yourself with thoughts about how you will achieve the goal — just focus on how great your confidence is going to feel for you when you have achieved it.

Here is another example of a goal-setting process, this time from David who wanted to become more confident with his body image.

STEP ONE

- **I always feel like I am not good enough and that there is something wrong with me.**

- **I feel like my confidence hits rock bottom when I put on weight.**

- **I don't like looking at myself in the mirror because I don't like what I see.**

- **I feel that nobody will ever love me if I don't lose some weight.**

- **I don't know if I can ever learn to feel better about myself.**

STEP TWO

I am starting to feel better about the way that I look. I recognize that beauty also comes from within and I can

do something to start to change my inner self-talk. I know that I usually work things out, so I just have to keep encouraging myself. I will be okay and can learn new habits that will support me. I like thinking about how good it will be when I start to feel confident about my body image. Won't it be great when I look in the mirror and like what I see?

Once you have written your goal and feel happy with it, I recommend you just read it once or twice a day for the next couple of weeks. Try reading it with a big smile on your face and feel how great it is going to be when you have achieved it. Again, don't worry about the detail of how it is going to happen; just focus on how good you will feel once it does happen!

TOP TIPS FOR WRITING CONFIDENCE GOALS

- **Focus on what you *do* want — not what you *don't* want.**

- **Keep your statements general. The more specific information you put in your goal, the more you may start to worry about how you are going to achieve it.**

- **Keep your goal to a few paragraphs.**

- **Make sure you write the goal based on how you would really like to feel — not how you think you should feel.**

- **Place your goal somewhere where you will remember to read it.**

- **Remember to smile when you are reading your goal and allow yourself to imagine how great your life will feel when you have achieved it.**

- **Don't worry if nagging doubts come into your head; just let them float on by and continue to read (and feel) your goal.**

- **Your goal is personal, so don't worry about getting the goal-setting exercise wrong.**

- **Make sure it feels good when you read it. If your goal feels too scary or unachievable, make your statements general, such as 'I am going to feel great when I feel confident,' rather than 'I feel really confident.'**

VISUALIZING CONFIDENCE

The technique of visualization — creating a picture or movie in your mind of what you would like to happen in your life — is nothing new. Sports people have been using it for years, and the good news is that it is also a very effective technique for confidence-building. However, as with goal-setting, I do want to stress that the aim is to *feel good* when you visualize rather than it being a process that you dread or feel you need to get done in order to complete this chapter ASAP. In order for visualization to work at its peak, it needs to be a feel-good process. When I do my own visualizations, I often add something funny, such as me doing a happy victory dance — this helps me lighten up and also stops me worrying how it is going to work or that it might not work at all.

Many celebrities have claimed that visualization has played a significant role in their success. Actor Will Smith used visualization to overcome challenges and, in fact, visualized his success years before he became successful. Other celebrities who have stated that visualization has worked for them include Jim Carrey, Oprah Winfrey, Tiger Woods and Arnold Schwarzenegger.

Research into brain function has shown that whenever we use visualization to imagine something happening, neurons in our brain interpret this as if we were doing something for real. New neural pathways are formed which, going forward, creates new programming that tells our mind to act according *to what we have imagined*. So, by taking the time to visualize something good happening, such as being assertive, standing up for ourselves, speaking in public or even feeling great on a hot date, we are actually activating the same neural networks in our head that we would if we were achieving the outcome in reality. Therefore, through visualization, we catch a glimpse of how we want our life to be — our preferred future rather than our current reality. When this happens, it gets the brain ready to go and create it and the body stores increased positive emotions about achieving the outcomes we desire.

I have come across many clients who avoid visualization. They often tell me that they are 'not a very visual person' or that they are no good at it. However, my response is to ask them what goes through their head when they are feeling scared and anxious or worrying about making a fool of themselves. Most of them realize they have been visualizing for years without knowing it and may have been automatically creating negative visualizations!

As with goal-setting, don't get hung up on making your visualization perfect — it should feel fun and light.

To assist you in visualizing confidence, you need to refer back to the goal you wrote earlier. You are going to visualize this goal actually taking place. In doing this, you are going to focus more on the end result, rather than getting bogged down in detail. You will be simply telling the unconscious mind what outcome you would like to create, rather than worrying about how or when it is going to happen.

As with goal-setting, there are no hard-and-fast rules, so just do what feels good to you. If you prefer a quiet space in which to visualize, then find one. However, I have had great success in fitting in a quick visualization for one minute while sitting on a bus or when the adverts are on TV. Just do what works for you as you follow the steps below.

Visualization process

Start by thinking about how you are going to look when you have achieved this goal. What does confidence look like in your visualization? Do you look calm and relaxed? How is your body language? Are your shoulders back and head up high? Are you looking proud, confident and self-assured?

If your goal contains statements such as, 'I feel confident in saying no' or perhaps being assertive with someone in particular, then run the scene in your head as you would like it to happen. Make sure you visualize the person nodding in agreement or accepting gracefully your needs and wants.

You can also involve all of your senses in your visualization, imagining how things smell or taste. Maybe you are celebrating that great speech by having a glass of champagne? Tune in to people saying positive things about you.

As with the goal, make sure you feel good about the scene in your head. Embrace the feeling of happiness now that you have a strong and hearty confidence muscle or you are easily being confident around other people.

When you are ready, just run this mental movie in your head a few times. Again, there is no right or wrong when it comes to visualization. Don't worry that you need to put in an Oscar-winning performance — just have fun with this technique and enjoy it!

TOP TIPS FOR GOAL-SETTING AND VISUALIZATION

- Always ensure your goals make you feel excited about achieving them.

- Don't worry about how your goal will come to fruition.

- Your goal and visualization should be tailored to what you want — rather than what you think you should do.

- Visualize as little or as often as you want — but only do it if it feels good.

CHAPTER 11

LEARNING TO BE ASSERTIVE

Assertiveness and confidence go hand in hand, and it is rather difficult to be confident without having a few practised assertiveness skills up your sleeve. In fact, if you don't learn assertiveness, you may find that your confidence is eaten away as you allow other people to violate your rights and take advantage of you. As children many of us received warped programming about being assertive, and as adults we might still be unconsciously copying or mirroring the passive or aggressive behaviour we saw from people around us. However, have faith, because in this chapter I will share some great assertiveness statements and techniques that will have you feeling powerful and confident in no time.

In Part One I wrote extensively about the importance of creating a mindset of safety. Therefore, if the mere thought of being assertive makes you shake in your boots, then this is an important action for you to do when building up your assertiveness skills. Don't forget to remind yourself that by learning assertive skills, you are learning to take care of yourself and take back your power — also, really, what is the worst that could happen? I also encourage you to read over the 'Personal Bill of Rights' chapter again and remind yourself that your ideas and opinions are as important as everyone else's. As with confidence, the foundations of assertiveness start with an inner attitude of valuing yourself just as much as you value others.

So, what does being assertive really mean? First of all let me explain what being assertive is *not*.

IT IS NOT BEING PASSIVE. A passive person allows other people to take control of their life and make decisions for them. They easily give their power away to others and don't often realize that they do have personal power. The passive person is usually that too-easy-going individual who ends up doing all the extra work in the office and just going along with what everyone else wants. It is the person who more often than not doesn't express their own opinion and appears to be happy fitting in with the crowd. Ever apologised for something that wasn't your fault? Yep, you've guessed it — that is also passive behaviour.

IT IS NOT BEING AGGRESSIVE. Being assertive is not about showing hostile, aggressive behaviour, which could include threatening other people or demanding things always go your way. It is not about storming off or shouting in order to be heard. Assertive behaviour does include standing up for your rights, but not in a way that violates the rights of other people.

IT IS NOT BEING PASSIVE–AGGRESSIVE. The passive–aggressive person can be hard to spot, because they use covert ways to control other people. I have to be honest here: if you have struggled with confidence for a long time, you may have used passive–aggressive behaviour to get your own way, because it is a technique born from fear of confrontation, hidden anger and an inability to deal straight with people.

Examples of passive–aggressive behaviour include:

- **Agreeing to do something and then doing the opposite.**

- **Seeing everything as a personal attack and even plotting revenge.**

- **Giving other people the silent treatment.**

- **Having to always have the last say by throwing in a final insult.**

> **'I didn't feel brave enough to tell my boss that I had too much work on, so instead I just made loads of mistakes and procrastinated so that he would finally get the message.' Philip, 36**

So, what *is* assertive behaviour?

For me, assertiveness is simply a communication style that allows me to clearly state how I wish to be treated by other people. Being assertive allows me to act in my own best interests and express my personal rights as a human being, without violating the rights of another human being. It allows me to place value on my own desires and to clearly ask for what I want. This includes requesting that other people treat me with respect.

When I am acting assertively, I also get that warm fuzzy feeling knowing that I am taking care of myself by listening to my body and honouring my needs and my emotions. This could mean feeling comfortable in declining other people's requests, pulling them up on their poor behaviour or simply saying 'no' if something doesn't work for me or I don't want to do something. It is about looking after my happiness and wellbeing and making sure that I place sufficient value on my life, my time and myself.

I acknowledge that it takes courage to be assertive — but believe me, some conversations need to be had and it is far better to speak up than hide your head in the sand hoping that things will just smooth over. Yes, it may feel scary at first, but in time you will find that being assertive is a better option than saying nothing and feeling awful or angry about something later on. Think back to a time when you were passive and swallowed your emotions or didn't speak up for yourself — how did it feel? Not good!

Please be aware that assertive behaviour doesn't mean that you will always get what you want — however, it is fair to say that it will bring you less of what you do *not* want. For me, one of the greatest gifts in being assertive is that with practice, it leaves you feeling empowered and confident in the knowledge that you have taken steps to speak up and take care of yourself. It's like sending a message to the world that, *Hey, I count and what I want is important!*

Assertive behaviour allows you to express yourself with confidence in a clear, open and reasonable way, without undermining the rights of yourself or others. It is a skill that can be used at home, work, with friends or even complete strangers.

Here are some different ways being assertive can assist you in specific areas of your life:

- **Relationships: Clearly expressing your feelings and being able to ask for what you want leads to healthier relationships, whether they are romantic or platonic.**

- **Career: Learning to be more assertive will open you up to get what you want in your career and increased job** satisfaction. If you are passive at work, the chances are you are undervalued and may also miss out on career advancement or promotion opportunities. Look at your own career — isn't it those who put themselves forward and who speak up get handed those great opportunities?

- **Family:** There are times when it is important to be assertive when dealing with family members, such as when asking them to do things for you or when making decisions. Of course, there will also be times when you need to have the courage to say 'no' to your family's requests.

- **Future success:** If you set yourself to change or focus on a goal, assertiveness is a useful tool in life because there will always be people who will try to dissuade you or stand in your way.

Unfortunately, many of us have been programmed to avoid being assertive because we make it mean that we are selfish — a belief I aim to change in each and every one of you. This is simply a misguided view and one that is often put upon you by the very people you need to be assertive with. The accurate view is that as long as you are stating your wishes calmly and confidently, you are not acting selfishly. Remember, you have a right to ask for what you want and what is right for you. This is your life, not anybody else's, so drive your own bus.

Another common blockage to assertiveness is the fear it may result in you hurting other people's feelings. I often challenge my clients on this myth by asking them: *Whose feelings are hurting right now?* It often comes as a surprise to people when they realize that they find hurting their own feelings far more acceptable than hurting anyone else's!

'I really wanted my flatmate to help me with the cleaning

around the house but was worried that he would get annoyed.' Travis, 35.

Fearing that people will react angrily to assertiveness is a common fear on the journey to confidence. Okay, this may be true for a few people but please don't assume that everyone is going to get upset or be unreasonable at your assertive behaviour. Remember, assertiveness is only asking to be treated as an equal, so if people don't accept this, are they the type of people you want to hang out with anyway? The reality is, most people will simply accept your point of view — you may be surprised how easily. Take a minute to think about those you know who are assertive. Do you think they are selfish? The chances are in fact that you respect them even more for being assertive, and this is true for you as well. People are more likely to think highly of you and respect you more for being assertive, because they will know exactly where they stand with you.

When you are building up your assertiveness skills, I find that it is a good idea to have a handful of statements ready to use for those rabbit-in-the-headlights moments. These are particularly useful for people who may find it difficult to say 'no' to other people's requests and often feel put on the spot and agree to do something they don't want to do. I recommend practising a few of these statements and have them ready for when you need them. Try these for a start:

- **Thank you for the offer, but that doesn't interest me right now.**
- **Thanks for asking, but I can't do that today.**
- **Thanks, but that isn't a priority for me at the moment.**
- **Thanks, but I have other plans — have fun!**

- **I would like to help, but this doesn't work for me right now.**

- **I will pass on this one.**

- **Thank you for thinking of me but I can't make it this time.**

- **I'll think about it and get back to you.**

- **I'm not sure about that. I will take some time to think about it and get back to you.**

START SMALL

Assertive techniques require practice, so don't dive in with big challenges first. Instead, start small with the least-risky ones. Practise being assertive with people you trust first of all, those you feel comfortable around, such as friends or family. If you find it difficult to ask for what you want, start by asking someone in your family to grab you a drink from the kitchen or a friend to save you a seat on the bus. Each time you do this, you will be building your confidence muscle. When you start to get the hang of it, move things up a notch, asking someone at the supermarket to help you find an item or request that someone at work give you some assistance with a task. The idea is to just get more comfortable in asking for what you want. Another benefit comes when you start to recognize that when you do ask for what you want, nothing terrible will actually happen. That fear is just in your mind.

You can build on this by also starting to get in some practice on stating your opinion. When someone asks your opinion on a topic, how do you usually react? Do you normally just nod and agree with someone else's opinion or do you speak up confidently and express your own individual view on the topic, even if it varies from the people around you?

Again, start with people you feel safe around, and have some fun with it. The more you state your opinion, the more you will learn to tap into what is important to you and your own personal preferences.

THE 'DON'T REALLY MIND' GAME

A great little fun game for building assertiveness is the 'Don't Really Mind' game. This involves writing down how many times a day you use the words 'I don't mind', or 'It's up to you', or 'I don't really care.' I do this with my clients and they are often shocked and dismayed when they realize they often do this unconsciously up to 95 per cent of the time! Okay, I know sometimes you really don't mind, particularly when it comes to things that you have little or no interest in, but going forward, wouldn't it be nice to be able to calmly state what you *do* want — especially when it is something of importance to you?

Play this game for a few days, making a note every time you simply state you have no preference. For many of us, it can be such a well-worn habit that we don't even realize when we do it.

Then, for fun, spend the next few days encouraging yourself to actually state your preferences. Again, just keep working on this until it feels more natural to you. Going forward, this will help you feel comfortable in stating your needs and wants to other people. For example, if someone asks you if you would like tea or coffee and your normal response would be, 'I don't mind, I'll have whatever you're having', get assertive and say, 'I would prefer a coffee, please.'

BUILDING UP ASSERTIVENESS

It is an inevitable fact of life that sometimes you just need to speak up and be heard. This could be asking your boss for a pay rise, requesting that a friend return the money they owe you, or declining to run around after a family member.

When you are aware that you will need to be assertive, it is great to prepare yourself and rehearse what you are going to say beforehand. You can use one of the assertive statements I shared on page 79 or put together a script of your own. Personally, I used to practise what I needed to say in front of the mirror as well as writing the words down on a piece of paper. Putting in this preparation time really helped me get crystal clear on what I wanted to say and less stressed about the whole situation. It also helps release fears of forgetting what you wanted to say if you worry you will panic or get sidetracked. If you choose to write your script on paper, there is also nothing wrong with taking this with you when you speak with someone. Set yourself up for success by using whatever resources you need to help you feel more comfortable.

PRACTISE USING 'I' STATEMENTS

Many of us put off being assertive because we fear a negative reaction from other people. We worry they may take it the 'wrong' way or become upset or angry. A good way to counteract this is by using 'I' statements. These are far softer and more powerful than hurling around blame statements such as, 'It's your fault that this is happening,' or 'You have really upset me.' Using a well-timed 'I' statement helps you say how you feel in a clear and concise way without expressing a judgement about the other person or blaming your feelings on anyone else. Remember, you always have a choice in the way you react.

Good 'I' statements include:

- **I would like you to respect my point of view.**
- **I feel offended by what you have said.**
- **I feel upset by what is happening and would like to discuss it with you so we can work it out.**
- **I didn't appreciate that remark.**

A good tip is to practise getting comfortable saying these statements out loud. This will help you feel more confident prior to having to use them when dealing with other people.

BROKEN-RECORD TECHNIQUE

In reality, most people will respect your boundaries and listen to what you have to say. However, if you find yourself dealing with someone who is pushy, won't listen to a word you say and continues to barrage you with interruptions or questions, then try the tested broken-record technique. This is a simple technique that involves repeating the same phrase over and over again in a calm relaxed way until the other person gets the message. Not only does it keep you on track with your words, it also prevents you getting sucked in to other people's dramas.

Here is an example of the broken-record technique:

Desna: *Can you lend me some money?*
Graham: *I can't lend you any money.*
Desna: *Please, Graham; I'll pay you back as soon as I can. I really need it desperately.*
Graham: *I can't lend you any money.*
Desna: *Why not? I know you have some, you've just been paid.*
Graham. *I can't lend you any money.*

Don't feel that you need to go into great detail explaining the reasons for your decision and justifying your response. If you do this, you may just find yourself digging yourself a deeper hole and losing hold of your assertiveness and giving in to their requests. Some people are master manipulators at this, so don't fall into the trap of trying to justify yourself. Just speak clearly and concisely, repeating the same message over and over again. Just because someone asks you to explain doesn't mean you have to respond!

KEEPING COOL, CALM AND COURAGEOUS

I know, easier said than done sometimes, but staying calm in any form of conflict always gives you an advantage. When you are upset or anxious, it is easy to fly off the handle, especially if you have been taken by surprise. However, the moment you start shouting or yelling insults, everything starts to go downhill and you may find yourself further and further away from what you really want. If you do find yourself getting angry (or of course if someone starts getting angry or shouting at you), then I highly recommend taking a few deep breaths and physically removing yourself from the situation you are in. This could mean walking into another room or taking a brief walk until you have calmed down. This is an act of self-care, and remember that you can always go back and discuss any outstanding issues at a later date, when emotions are less fiery.

If someone else gets heated up and angry, a great assertive statement for you to use is, 'I am not going to continue this conversation until you calm down,' or 'I can see you are upset, so I am going to leave this conversation until you are ready to speak calmly.' Again, this takes courage but always remember that you don't have to allow someone else to dump their bad mood on you — you can always take back your power and remove yourself from the situation. Again, this is a good act of self-care and valuing yourself.

TOP TIPS FOR ASSERTIVENESS

- Being assertive takes courage, so first create your mindset of safety.

- Be patient with yourself. Remember that you will sometimes be better at it than at other times, but you can always learn from your mistakes.

- Remind yourself that a difference of opinion is healthy and sometimes you may just need to agree to disagree.

- Don't apologize for things when you don't need to.

- Being assertive shows the world that you care about yourself and that you respect your own needs.

CHAPTER 12

CONFIDENCE AFFIRMATIONS

A ffirmations — you either love them or you hate them, but done properly they are a great way to build up your confidence muscle from the inside out. They are simply self-instructions that you repeat in your mind (or you can say them out loud if you wish) that focus on how you want to feel or an end result you would like to create, such as a new behaviour pattern, a positive new emotion or even a new relationship. They are usually concise statements made in the first person.

When consciously choosing to practise affirmations you are actually re-programming your mind with new healthy thoughts that serve the wonderful person you are today.

As highlighted in Part One, if we received lots of negative pro-gramming in the past, our minds tend to automatically fire up negative thoughts, many of which we are simply not aware of. We actually fire up anywhere between 12,000 and 60,000 thoughts a day. What I find more interesting, though, is that psychologists have found that 98–99 per cent of our thoughts are repeated each day and over 80 per cent of these are negative — that's 80 per cent of the thoughts we think that could be eating away at our confidence and self-esteem!

The good news is that we can consciously choose to replace some of these negative thoughts using positive affirmations. When used regularly, these affirmations will re-program your brain with new positive thoughts and beliefs. I have been a fan of affirmations for many years and have used them with success in my personal and professional life. However, I strongly recommend that you begin with affirmations that don't feel too much of a stretch for you at first and that make you feel excited. Many books on self-development advise you to choose an affirmation that simply states how you would like to feel and often begin with the words 'I am'. For example: 'I am more confident,' 'I am worthy,' 'I deserve.' Although this approach does work for many people, in my experience it can have the opposite effect — for some people it causes more self-doubt to rise to the surface because they just can't imagine it ever happening for them. Another downside is that if it doesn't feel good, you may just give up on the affirmation altogether.

Therefore, in order to build confidence, we will be working with affirmations that create excitement in you, and are not too much of a stretch for you to believe.

JANE

Jane felt very nervous when meeting new people. She worked in a large marketing department, so she found that this fear was really holding her back in her career. Jane found herself growing anxious and worrying that she would say something stupid, and as a result she often stumbled

over her words and ended up feeling flustered. She constantly found herself on the outside of conversations wishing she had more confidence to just join in and have fun. As part of the coaching process with Jane, we looked at using a couple of simple affirmations that would help shift some of the well-worn negative programming she had running in her mind on auto-pilot.

Having felt like this for many years, Jane had a lot of self-doubt and didn't believe she could solve this issue. Although she had a strong desire to become more confident, she really doubted her ability to actually do something about it. I worked with Jane to start to change her mindset, and she began to use more encouraging and supportive thoughts whenever she felt anxious or scared. In addition, I introduced affirmations to Jane and we worked on finding the right affirmation for her.

First of all, I asked Jane to say out loud the affirmation 'I am confident,' and then give feedback on a scale of one to ten of how much she actually believed it. As Jane had suffered from a lack of confidence from an early age, she reported that the statement didn't feel believable for her; it just didn't feel right in her body. In actual fact, when she repeated it again it had the negative effect of making her feel even worse, causing her mind to bring forward even more negative thoughts such as 'That will never happen,' or 'That affirmation is just not true for me.' As a result, despite her strong desire to become more confident, she only rated this affirmation a two out of ten on the believable scale.

So, we moved on to find an affirmation that felt higher up the scale for Jane. I asked her to try saying the affirmation: 'I am really looking forward to becoming more confident.' Jane was surprised to tell me that, in fact, this felt far more believable to her, and as a result she rated it as five out of ten. Good news!

My aim was to find Jane an affirmation that not only was believable for her, but that also felt good when she said it.

Jane then tried another new affirmation: 'Wouldn't it be nice if I could feel more confident?' I could actually see Jane become more relaxed and confident with this statement and she seemed to lighten up immediately and enjoy saying it. The good news is that she rated it as eight out of ten on the scale. Jane also told me that it just felt more believable to her and made her feel more positive about becoming the confident person she really wanted to be. Importantly, Jane felt motivated to start working with this great affirmation.

To summarize, affirmations are a great tool in building up your confidence, but it is important to start with one that feels good for you. Do you remember in the chapter on goal-setting I mentioned the importance of setting a goal that feels good? Well, this concept is the same for affirmations. I have found that the key factor in making affirmations really work is to choose one that makes you feel good and you enjoy using.

Once you have been using the same affirmation for a while, you can then move on to another one, but always check in with your body to see how comfortable it feels for you. Trust your own judgement on this — we are all unique, and affirmations will feel different to each one of us. Below, I have highlighted some confidence affirmations for you to try on for size. Just choose one to begin with and work with it until it almost feels boring to you. Then move on to find another one that feels great.

Try starting with one of these:

- **It is safe for me to start to think about becoming more confident.**

- **I would really like to feel more confident.**
- **Wouldn't it be nice if I could start to build up my confidence muscle?**
- **It is going to feel really good when I start to feel more confident.**
- **I am really looking forward to feeling more confident.**

When you are ready, you can move on to more direct statements such as:

- **I am becoming more confident every day.**
- **It feels really good to be building up my confidence.**
- **I really like feeling assertive and confident.**
- **I am a confident person.**

Again, have fun with your affirmations. If you find one that you like, begin repeating it at least ten times a day. Ideally, start in the morning if you can — you could even do them in the shower or place a piece of paper with an affirmation written on it on your bathroom mirror to remind you to do it each morning. I do mine when I am doing the housework and it really passes the time!

TOP TIPS FOR AFFIRMATIONS

- Choose an affirmation that you enjoy repeating and that feels good.

- Develop a routine for repeating your affirmations; it could be first thing in the morning, while you are taking a shower, or as you wait for a bus.

- Try downloading affirmations from the web onto your MP3 player and listen to them regularly.

- Keep the affirmations short and sweet and easy to remember.

CHAPTER 13

WHAT DO YOU LIKE ABOUT YOU?

After coaching thousands of wonderful people over the years, I have come to believe that human beings are their own worst enemies. We often treat other people far better than we treat ourselves and are more at home beating ourselves up mentally and emotionally than we are in actually being nice to ourselves.

So far in this book I have discussed numerous methods to build confidence, but one thing that can propel you to new heights of confidence is something quite simple: putting a bit of effort into liking yourself a little bit more. This really is a rewarding and important step.

If I asked you now to tell me five things you don't like about yourself, I am sure you could reel them off without even stopping to take a breath — in fact, you probably wouldn't even stop at five.

However, what if I asked you to share five things that you liked about yourself — how would you react? Would you be able to do this easily or would you look at me as if I had gone mad and struggle to come up with even one thing? Would you feel embarrassed or feel that being nice to yourself is unacceptable in some way?

Don't worry, you are not alone; most people usually look at me in shock when I ask them to do this exercise.

Let's be completely honest here. What thoughts go through your head when you look in the mirror? What do you tell yourself when you are getting ready for a night out or to meet new people for the first time? When you lie in bed at night, what do you tell yourself?

Are your thoughts filled with kindness or contempt? Think back over the past week: have you said or thought even one nice thing about yourself? When was the last time you gave yourself a pat on the back for a job well done? When was the last time you sat for a minute and really appreciated yourself for how far you have come in doing the exercises in this book? When was the last time you thanked yourself for doing something nice for yourself or taking care of your own needs?

> **'I would look like a perfectly happy person all day at work but as soon as I got home all I would think about was what a failure I was.' Martin, 35**

Human beings are their own critics and worst enemies. I am sure if you spoke to your friends the way you speak to yourself, they wouldn't choose to hang out with you. And yet we seem to think it is perfectly acceptable to criticize, punish, scorn and put down our own selves. In my twelve years as a coach I have never had a client say that they feel better after beating themselves up — so why do we continue to do it?

I often start my coaching sessions by reminding clients that they are not broken nor do they have a fatal flaw. I tell them they are perfectly lovely human beings doing the best they can with the resources they currently have. At first, most don't believe me but this is true for each and every one of them — and for you. It's about time you gave yourself a break and started to see yourself through kinder eyes.

You deserve to have a great life and to treat yourself with respect. It really doesn't matter what you think you may have done wrong in the past, you deserve your own forgiveness and you deserve to be happy. Despite the programming you may have received, you are worthy, wonderful and loveable and there is nothing wrong with you. Yes, you may have been programmed to believe that you are a failure but this simply isn't true. You are magnificent — each and every one of you.

I can see it, and I would like you to see it within yourself.

It is time for you to take back your power and start to like yourself a little bit more. You owe this to yourself even if it takes a bit of effort. It doesn't matter where your life is at the moment, you can begin to take a few steps towards learning to like yourself more. It really is one of the most important things you can do for yourself.

Learning to like who you are comes with a truckload of benefits and no downside. Not only will your body and mind feel nicer to live in, but your life will feel far more fun and relaxing and your health will also improve. You will also bounce back quickly from life's unexpected challenges and find it much easier to be assertive and let your confidence shine.

Can you imagine how much easier you would find it to speak up and ask for what you want if you truly believed you deserved it? Think back to a situation where you have been unhappy, whether it is in your professional or private life — do you think you would have dealt with this situation differently if you cared more about yourself? Would you continue to put up with a negative situation or one that makes you miserable if you really liked and respected who you are? The truth is that when you start to like who you are, caring about your life and emotional wellbeing becomes a priority and you will find yourself less likely to put up with any person or situation that makes you unhappy.

> **'You yourself, as much as anybody in the entire universe deserve your love and affection.' Buddha**

One of the most transformational times in my life was when I spent four years in an abusive relationship. During this time, my self-esteem and confidence hit rock bottom and I hated my life and myself. What really made a difference was learning to like myself a little bit more. You see, when I liked myself, I no longer expected myself to stay in this relationship or tolerate cruel behaviour from my partner. When I liked myself, I started to see that I needed to look after my own emotional wellbeing more. When I liked myself, I cared enough about myself to walk away from this unhealthy relationship, because I knew I deserved better.

Several months after the relationship ended, I took the time to write down what liking myself had enabled me to do in my life, and this is what my list looked like:

- **I learned to speak up for myself and honour my feelings. In liking myself I realized that I no longer needed to just go along with what other people wanted.**

- **I learned to put myself first and be selfish sometimes. If I don't take care of my own needs, then who will?**

- **I learned to treat myself with kind words and encouragement. I am only human, at the end of the day, so there really is no need to beat myself up for making mistakes. Mistakes only require correction, not punishment.**

- **I learned to stop tolerating poor or disrespectful behaviour from other people. (This was a big one for me.) Learning to like myself included giving myself permission to walk away from people who continually hurt me.**

- **I learned to be assertive and stand up for myself.**

- **I learned how to put good boundaries in place and teach other people how I would like to be treated.**

- **I learned to give myself plenty of rest and relaxation time.**

- **I learned to be my own cheerleader.**

- **I learned to have compassion for myself.**

- **I learned to embrace encouraging thoughts — no beating myself up!**

So, how can you start to like yourself a little bit more? Follow me and I will share my most effective tips.

As with affirmations, a good place to start is to consciously take the time to embed new healthy thoughts and programs into your mind. One of the most simple and effective ways I have found of doing this is to begin writing in a 'self-love journal'. This can be a simple notebook or perhaps you may want to treat yourself to a new hardback journal.

The purpose of the journal is for you to write down, every day if you can, at least two things you like about yourself. This could be your hair, the colour of your eyes or maybe the fact that you are a kind, loving person. Perhaps you are rather fond of your cooking skills. Maybe you are helpful, funny or a good driver? It can be anything at all — but you need to write down at least two things each day.

Most people find this difficult, because it may be the first time in years they have thought about being nice to themselves. Try not to fall into the trap of having to find a major thing to write down in your journal, just choose simple traits or habits or whatever you find pleasing about yourself. The important thing is to be consistent and try to write at least two each day. It is fine if you find yourself repeating the same trait. If you struggle with this or find yourself drawing a blank, you can also use things you feel you have done well each day. It could be something as simple as getting to work on time or repeating your affirmations in the shower. It could be that you cleaned your teeth or got the kids off to school on time. Continue with this practice for at least two months and I promise you: your life will change. An additional benefit of this process is that if you are having a down day or feeling miserable, you can simply spend five minutes re-reading your journal in order to give yourself a timely confidence boost.

Another great way to assist you in starting to like who you are a little more, is to practise giving yourself some well-deserved self-praise. Again, it is not unusual for people to find this difficult, because they may have been brought up with the belief that self-praise is arrogant or that they don't deserve their own praise. However, praising yourself is a great way to boost that confidence muscle — and also, it really does feel nice to blow your own trumpet!

To get into the habit of this, why not commit to praising yourself once a day, when you look in the mirror? Most of us are more likely to put ourselves down or say something insulting rather than positive when faced with the mirror, so it is the perfect place to inject a little more praise into your day. At first, getting into the habit of saying something good about yourself can feel difficult, but don't give up — surely you owe yourself a few minutes a day to take care of yourself?

You really can't get this process wrong, and your self-praise can be about anything at all. I must admit, this exercise is really one of my favourites because I have seen the changes it can make to a person's confidence. I know it takes a bit of practice at first but it really is worth it!

CASE STUDY

AMANDA

Amanda had been working on her confidence muscle for several weeks when I suggested that she started to praise herself each time she looked in the mirror.

'No way!' she exclaimed. 'What have I done to deserve my own praise?' I then discussed with Amanda what she felt she needed to achieve before she felt worthy of her own praise. 'Oh,' she said, 'something big, like passing my driving test or an exam.'

Can you see how the way Amanda had set herself up made it very difficult for her to praise herself? She needed to do something totally amazing for her to say a kind word about herself.

I then shared with Amanda the achievements that I had praised myself for that same morning. They included the following:

- I got out of bed on time.
- I brushed my teeth and had a shower.
- I cooked myself a healthy breakfast.
- I said my affirmations.
- I placed my dirty dishes in the dishwasher.

Amanda was shocked that I praised myself for getting out of bed. 'Why not', I said — 'I deserve my own praise. I like myself!'

Here is what Amanda said after doing this action step for a couple of weeks:

'I really didn't want to do this exercise. It felt stupid praising myself for just cleaning my teeth or having a shower. I wasn't happy about doing it. Then, after about a week, I realized how nice it felt to be con-gratulating myself and I was starting to feel I deserved it. A month on, I am happy to do this exercise because it really has had a positive impact on how I feel about myself.'

There are hundreds of other things you can do in order to start to like yourself a little bit more. Here are a few additional action steps that you may wish to try:

- **Look in the mirror and affirm, 'It would be nice if I could be kinder to myself.'**

- **Ask five close friends for a list of what they like about you and write the answers in your love journal.**

- **Each day, choose to do one thing that is kind and nurturing for yourself rather than for other people.**

- **Make a list of twenty things that make you happy, and try to do at least one a day.**

- **Take some time out to relax and rewind even if it is for only ten minutes a day.**

TOP TIPS TO LIKING YOURSELF

- **Acknowledge that you are just as worthy as everyone else in this world and deserve your own love and attention.**

- **Learning to like yourself is one of the most valuable things you can do for yourself.**

- **For many people, this is the most difficult chapter of this book — remember that this can often mean you will reap huge rewards by persisting with the suggested actions.**

- **Discipline your mind and encourage yourself to practise these steps consistently — even if you don't feel like it.**

- **Never beat yourself up if you find these actions difficult. Return to finding a soothing and supportive mindset. You can do it — I promise you.**

When used consistently, the techniques I have shared with you in this section will ensure that your confidence muscle remains a healthy and integrated part of your future. Also, don't forget that goal-setting and visualization are tools you can use throughout your life, whether it is to increase confidence, create a new career or relationship, or resolve a difficult situation.

Please don't underestimate the power of learning to like yourself. Ideally, try to incorporate this practice into your day for the rest of your life. Liking yourself really is an essential part of your personal growth and will ensure that you develop healthy and happy relationships with yourself and other people.

PART THREE

Confidence in Specific Situations

CHAPTER 14

CONFIDENCE IN PUBLIC SPEAKING

Numerous studies have shown that over 73 per cent of the population has a fear of public speaking — and apparently, some people fear it more than death itself. Jerry Seinfeld interpreted this as meaning that at a funeral, more people would rather be in the casket than giving the eulogy.

The phobia of public speaking is real and can range from slight nervousness, to a paralysing feeling of fear and panic. It is not just the fear of making a fool of yourself, being judged or forgetting your words that might hold you back from being a great speaker; you might also fear your own physical reaction, which for some, results in a shaking voice, blushing or even trembling hands.

Many people avoid public speaking at all costs, going out of their way to not pursue careers or situations that could involve standing up and taking the stage in front of others. In doing so, they may keep themselves in careers or experiences that they deem as being 'safe', often passing up opportunities for promotion. I know of a few people who deliberately take a day off work, get sick or arrive late to a meeting in the hope that they miss out on even those dreaded customary introductions ('Let's go round the table and introduce ourselves.'). Although these avoidance techniques provide immediate relief they are not a long-term solution.

Public speaking, whether it is standing up at a conference, presenting at work, facilitating a team meeting or giving the best-man's speech, really doesn't need to be the frightening experience we believe it to be. In this chapter, we will explore the different steps you can take to build up your public-speaking confidence muscle. Think of this journey just like learning how to ride a bike — you may feel a bit wobbly at first but after time you will gradually find it much easier. In my experience, people who have struggled with public speaking for years do successfully learn to control their fears and many end up really enjoying speaking in public!

GOAL-SETTING AND VISUALIZATION

Do you find that your mind gets so bogged down in what could go wrong with the act of public speaking that you don't even consider what could go right? Have you ever taken the time to encourage yourself to try it or consider that you might actually be rather good at it or even enjoy it? It is time to shift your mind to focus on how great it will feel when you do actually overcome the fear of public speaking.

In Part Two we discussed the simple process for goal-setting and visualization, and it is time to build on these skills. When constructing a public-speaking goal, don't forget to focus on how proud you will feel when you have broken free from your fears and mastered the art of public speaking. (If you need to refresh your mind on the goal-setting and visualization process, skip back and read pages 64 to 73 again.)

Once you have written your goal, spend a few minutes visualizing yourself looking confident and relaxed. You may even want to picture the audience giving you a standing ovation.

These two simple steps will open your mind to possibility and start to create new neuro pathways in your brain, which allow new ways of thinking and habits to form. In time, new positive feelings about public speaking will also be created, which will make it easier for you to learn new behaviours and attitudes. Again, don't spend any time worrying about how the goal will eventually happen, just have some fun with it and make sure the goal you have written feels good to you.

JOHN

CASE STUDY

John was successful at work, but he feared stepping up to a managerial role because he realized he would have to facilitate team meetings and also present his sales figures to the rest of the management team on a monthly basis. This fear literally kept John stuck on his career path and left him feeling very frustrated.

After allowing this fear to hold him back for many years, John became determined to make a change. His dream was really just to be able to feel relaxed and confident about public speaking whether it was in front of a small or large group. When John wrote his goal for public speaking, it looked like this:

I am really looking forward to feeling confident and comfortable when I stand up and talk in front of people. I know that I can learn to feel better about doing this and things will get easier every time I try. It feels really good thinking about how good it will feel when I am standing up on stage and the words are just flowing easily out of my mouth and my body feels relaxed and happy.

After writing his goal, John also took some time to visualize a picture of himself standing confidently on stage. In his mind's eye, he imagined himself standing tall and speaking with ease and flow, with the audience laughing away with him. He also imagined himself with a big smile on his face and really enjoying the experience.

As he visualized, John started to feel excited about public speaking for the first time because he was more focused on how great it would feel, rather than on all the things that could possibly go wrong.

MINDSET

Arming yourself with a positive and supportive mindset will help you become a confident speaker. Yes, I acknowledge that this can be a challenge to those who have dreaded pubic speaking for most of their life, but remember that this is simply a well-worn negative pattern that you have been running on for many years. You have got into the habit of thinking more scary thoughts than supportive ones, often as a result of negative programming or just listening to other people's negative experiences.

In my opinion, a supportive mindset is something that will ultimately win you confidence as a speaker — however, please remember that it often needs to be nurtured gradually over time, so have patience with yourself.

Let's begin by looking at some of the negative or unsupportive thoughts that are common when people think about public speaking. Does any of this sound familiar to you?

- **Everyone will be looking at me and I will make a fool of myself.**
- **Other people will laugh at me.**
- **I will shake and won't be able to speak and other people will notice.**

- **I feel like everyone is judging me.**

- **My colleagues are really good at public speaking and I am terrible.**

- **I feel ashamed that I feel like this — what if I have a panic attack on stage?**

- **I will give a really terrible speech and everyone will know — I will be a laughing stock.**

When you allow these thoughts to hijack your mind, it eats away at your confidence and creates a body and mind filled with stress and anxiety. You might experience stress symptoms weeks before you are due to set foot on stage and these feelings might get stronger as the date of the event gets closer. As a result, the mere thought of the event has so much power over you that you end up fully expecting the worst to happen and assume that you will inevitably fail.

ACTION STEP

Write in your journal any emotional and physical symptoms you encounter prior to public speaking.

In order to reduce the chance of these symptoms occurring, it is important to set your mindset up to be one that will encourage you into success, rather than doom you to failure.

After John had enjoyed the process of visualizing his new public-speaking goal, I worked with him on creating a mindset that would help him feel safe and less stressed and provide him with valuable reassurance. John was quite resistant at first because he had convinced himself that he was going to fail and that people would laugh at him. These thoughts had paralyzed

John for years and prevented him from taking any action to change things. He simply didn't want to take the risk of embarrassing himself.

I reminded John that the best way to create safety in his own mind was to spend some time finding soothing and encouraging words, in the same way he would encourage a small child. As a result, John came up with the following phrases that he felt would support him:

- **Although I feel really nervous, I know I will be okay; I just need to do the best that I can.**

- **What evidence do I have that all my fears will actually become reality?**

- **I am going to make sure that I prepare well and give it a go. I have overcome fears in the past and remember how good it felt; I am sure I can do it again.**

- **It's okay, I don't need to be perfect first time; I just need to do my best; that's all I can do right now.**

- **I know I feel concerned that people may judge me but in reality, I am not a mind reader, so I am going to give up worrying about what they think. (I reminded John that in actual fact, the majority of his audience would also be scared of public speaking so they were more likely to think that John was really brave!)**

- **I will be okay; other people have done it and I am sure they felt scared at some time as well. I have achieved lots of good things in the past and I can do this as well.**

During the next few weeks, if John noticed worrying or negative thoughts creeping into his mind about speaking in public, he would switch to focusing his thoughts on soothing himself into feeling better and creating relief by repeating these phrases. At first, he admitted he found this quite difficult, because his mind ran automatically with the old programming. However, after focusing for several weeks, John found it much easier and started to feel much more relaxed and, importantly, more confident in successfully achieving his goal.

ACTION STEP

- Take a few minutes to think about your fear of public speaking. What do you fear the most?

- Create some new soothing statements or thoughts that you can use to build up your public-speaking confidence muscle.

- Whenever a scary thought comes to mind, focus on soothing yourself with your new statements.

TOP TIPS FOR A SUPPORTIVE MINDSET

- You are starting to replace old thoughts you may have had for years, so be patient with yourself. Don't expect your thoughts to change overnight. If you can start to soothe yourself several times a week, then this is a great start.

- Never give up on or get angry with yourself if you feel that nothing is changing. Have patience.

- Use encouraging and soothing words to encourage yourself to practise encouraging and soothing words!

- Remind yourself that any time you do something new, it is always going to feel a little uncomfortable.

THE PROBLEM WITH PERFECTIONISM

Although I acknowledge that ultimately your goal is to become a super-duper confident public speaker, setting your expectations too high at first can do your confidence muscle more harm than good. Yes, it is important to always strive to do your best and encourage yourself to do new things, but if you are one of those perfectionists who gives yourself a hard time for not always being 'perfect' enough, then you are setting yourself up for even more stress and anxiety.

Even great speakers such as Martin Luther King and Winston Churchill had numerous errors in their most famous speeches, so it is important to recognize that it is perfectly acceptable and normal to make mistakes and your first few attempts at public speaking may not always be perfect.

Perfectionists often have the following traits and behaviours:

- **Setting themselves high expectations to meet and beating themselves up when they believe they have not met these expectations.**

- **Dedicating a large amount of time and effort to make sure things are 'just right'.**

- **Constantly pushing themselves to always 'do better' or achieve more.**

- **Worrying about their shortcomings, believing they are not good enough.**

- **When they don't receive the ideal state of perfection, they experience negative emotions such as guilt, anxiety, frustration and sadness.**

I know that it sounds ironic, but perfectionism can literally stop you from enjoying simple achievements and prevent you from gracefully stepping into greatness.

'When I was practising my public-speaking skills, I expected myself to be perfect. If I made a mistake, stumbled over my words or didn't do everything 100 per cent right, I would automatically think I had not done a good enough job and that I was always going to be a terrible speaker.' Peter, 47

Perfectionists take minor mistakes and build them up into personal failures. They take to heart any sort of perceived shortcomings in their speaking technique and are never satisfied that they have done their best. In order for a perfectionist to feel successful, they often need to at least meet or exceed their own high expectations.

ANNA

Anna was a bit of a perfectionist and in her mind anything less than 100 per cent simply wasn't good enough. During her first experience of public speaking in front of twenty people, she mixed her words up several times and also felt her hands shaking. Once she had completed her speech, instead of focusing on how well she had done and giving herself some well-deserved self-praise, Anna got really down on herself, labelling herself a loser and beating herself up for making silly mistakes.

Can you understand how Anna had set things up to make it virtually impossible to make herself feel good about her first attempt at public speaking? Although by most people's standards she was doing really well, in her own mind it didn't matter how much she tried or how much effort she put into public speaking, she would rarely meet her own expectations.

We are literally our own worst enemies — often being kinder to other people, even strangers, than we are to ourselves. We criticize ourselves endlessly for not being perfect, and more often than not we focus on the things we believe we have done wrong, rather than the things we have done right.

In order to build up your confidence muscle for public speaking, it's important to give yourself a break. See your journey into becoming a great public speaker as work in progress rather than something you have to perfect straightaway. The truth is that as a human being, you are not going to always get things right 100 per cent of the time and it is far more beneficial to take an attitude of kindness and compassion with yourself than it is to beat yourself up.

The next time Anna took to the stage, her expectations were a little more realistic as she acknowledged to herself that she was bound to make a few mistakes because she was just starting out and learning new public-speaking skills.

As a result, she was far more relaxed on the stage and her words flowed effortlessly. Yes, she still shook a bit and forgot a few of her words but overall Anna felt really positive about her first big step into public speaking. Importantly, after the presentation was complete, Anna spent a few minutes focusing on all the things that she had done well and gave herself some well-deserved praise for even getting on the stage in the first place.

TIPS FOR REDUCING PERFECTIONISM

- **Remind yourself that you are learning new habits and skills, therefore it is somewhat ridiculous to expect yourself to get it right the first time.**

- **Laugh at the high expectations you set yourself.**

- **Replace perfectionist thoughts with realistic ones.**

- **After doing anything new, praise yourself for giving it a try and focus on the positives, not the negatives.**

- **Give yourself a break!**

Are you beginning to realize that giving yourself a hard time, believing those negative thoughts and being a perfectionist are the very things that just may be preventing you from being a confident speaker? If you do want to feel great about public speaking, the key thing is to learn to treat yourself kindly and with compassion — whatever stage you are at in public-speaking mastery.

PRACTICAL TIPS FOR PUBLIC SPEAKING

So far in this chapter we have focused on building a confident mindset and the importance of supporting yourself. For the rest of the chapter we will look at some of the more practical tips to public speaking.

Preparation

If you know your stuff in advance, you will be well on your way to setting yourself up for success and improving your public-speaking confidence. Don't allow your fears to cause you to procrastinate or hold you back from giving yourself sufficient time to prepare; bite the bullet, go for it and of course don't forget to use encouraging thoughts to remind yourself that you will be fine.

Always make sure you get to the location or venue early so you can check out the room in a relaxed way — you can also make sure that all the technical equipment is working.

If you are lucky enough to be able to choose a topic to speak about, aim for something you are passionate about and that makes you feel good. When you present, your energy will be infectious and people will pick up on your enthusiasm and be more interested in what you have to say.

If your topic has been chosen for you, don't be scared to make it uniquely yours; tell stories and bring your personality into the topic. Telling a good story in a presentation can really help connect you to your audience and also enables you to tell the audience a little bit about yourself.

The night before your speech, also make sure you get a good night's sleep. You could even try listening to some relaxing music or meditating to chill you out even more.

Practise, practise, practise!

I am sure you have heard this before, but practising your presentation beforehand will boost your confidence on the day. Even experienced speakers rehearse their speeches many times to make sure their brain becomes familiar with the words and to set themselves up to deliver a successful live performance. One of my personal tips is to stand in front of a mirror while practising. Most people dislike looking at themselves in the mirror, so if you can get comfortable in this process, speaking in front of others will feel a little less daunting.

When I was just starting out in my own speaker career, I made sure I was armed with a good selection of visual aids such as presentation slides to help trigger my memory. Although you may fear giving a 'death by PowerPoint' speech, don't hold back from writing down key words or triggers on your slides if you think it will help you. Having a visual for your audience to look at will also reassure you that people are not just staring straight at you. Even the thought of giving a speech to people who are not looking at you is always easier.

I also find that memorizing the first few lines of my presentation always helps me to feel more confident at the beginning of a presenta-tion, especially while I am just getting comfortable on stage or getting used to the equipment and microphone.

Learn to be yourself

Allowing yourself to be authentic on stage will help you relax, have fun and be more confident. Don't try to be something you are not, because people will see straight through you — and let's face it, trying to be something you are not often feels awkward anyway.

Being honest about your skills is a tip that has also served me well. I am often asked to speak at, or chair, conferences where I know little about either the organization or the other topics in the conference. Of course I do my preparation but there are times when the subject matter is rather technical or I am the only speaker covering a 'soft skills' topic such as confidence. As a result, I usually admit my lack of technical knowledge early on and it is interesting to see the audience warm to me, often laughing with me when I make a pronunciation mistake or am unable to answer a technical question.

I really encourage you to take an honest and authentic approach with your audience. If you are feeling nervous, just admit it! This will help you relax and, importantly, have your audience supporting you in doing well. Also, imagine their surprise when you give them a great presentation despite your nervousness.

Speak to one person at a time

For some people, the most terrifying thing about public speaking is thinking about the audience. I have found that what can often help is to pick someone in the audience and imagine you are talking only with them, as if there were nobody else in the room. If someone does ask you a question, you can simply change your focus to them in order to answer the question.

Imagine yourself succeeding

Even if you have already completed the visualization action step, do this each time before you speak. Imagine yourself giving a great speech, with everything going really well. Also conjure those feelings of pleasure and pride in yourself when you have finished. Learn to visualize success and your body will follow suit.

Dress confidently

Look your best. Take some time with your appearance and wear clothes in which you feel comfortable and professional. If you are happy with your appearance, you will feel more confident.

Remember to breathe

If you feel anxious, it is perfectly okay to stop for a few moments and take a breath. I often have a glass of water on stage for those times, and I find it really helps me to slowly drink some water and catch my breath. This gives me sufficient time to ground myself and get back on track.

To summarize, you are the person who can make your journey to public speaking as easy or as difficult as you choose. You can choose to frighten yourself and convince yourself you are going to fail, or you can choose to set yourself up for success by setting realistic expectations. You also have the choice to focus on your mistakes or give yourself a well-deserved pat on the back for doing your best, even if things did not work out perfectly.

TOP TIPS FOR CONFIDENT PUBLIC SPEAKING

- **Remember that contrary to what your mind may trick you into thinking, nobody is sitting in the audience laughing at you or waiting for you to make a mistake. People are not judging you negatively and more often than not, your audience is on your side. They have no plans to laugh at you, put you down or label you as a failure. Honestly, the only person who does this to you is you!**

- **If you do make a mistake, just let it go and move on. I often laugh with my audience every time I make an error, and so far I have never met an audience that hasn't laughed with** me. In fact, the fact that I wasn't 'perfect' at public speaking often became my icebreaker after various experiences of tripping over my microphone, being unable to pronounce a long word or my slides mysteriously disappearing from the screen!

- Remind yourself of the question: What is the worst that could happen if you are not perfect? Also, remember that in most cases, nobody will even notice if you slip up.

- Always take the time to praise yourself for progress, even when progress is small.

- Allow your authentic self to come out and relax. If you try too hard, you are more likely to make mistakes. Enjoy it and have fun.

- Learn to laugh at yourself. The best public speakers know that making mistakes is inevitable. Malfunctioning technology and forgetting lines are all part of the process.

CHAPTER 15

CONFIDENCE WITH BULLIES

There really is no simple definition of bullying because it can take so many forms, from the boss who shouts at you in front of others, to a mother-in-law who criticizes your parenting style or a partner who consistently puts you down about your dress sense or weight.

In general terms, bullying means one person, or group of persons, being rude or cruel to, teasing or deliberately upsetting, another person or group. Unlike bullying at school, adult bullies can be difficult to spot — they can be manipulative and sly, leaving you feeling like you are going crazy. Unfortunately, many people don't realize that they are being bullied, preferring to label themselves as 'too sensitive' or making excuses for another person's poor behaviour by convincing themselves that 'they didn't really mean it'. Research by the Australian Industry Group has shown an increase in workplace bullies in the form of colleagues, supervisors or management who hide behind masks of authority. One thing remains: whatever form the bullying takes, it can be a devastating experience for the victim.

Bullies are predators who seek out individuals with low confidence. They often choose targets who are capable, popular, intelligent and attractive but whose interpersonal style tends to be non-confrontational. Most victims of bullies have little self-confidence to begin with, and this is quickly diminished further when faced with obvious or even covert attacks from bullies, manipulators and abusers.

It is an understandable and common response for victims of bullying to blame themselves. Rather than looking objectively at the bully's bad behaviour they often turn inwards, asking themselves if they are responsible in some way through their words or actions. Trying to work out why a bully acts the way they do can then cause the victim unnecessary frustration and lower their confidence even more, so if this sounds like you, do yourself a favour and try not to blame yourself.

Remember, a bully's bad behaviour is entirely their own responsibility — not that of their target. If you feel that you are being bullied, make sure you regularly remind yourself that you didn't 'ask for it', nor is the bully's behaviour your fault. As human beings, we were all born with free will and we can't actually make anyone do anything. The only responsibility you have when being bullied is to take care of yourself and your emotional wellbeing and protect yourself from this toxic behaviour. Remember, it is your personal right to be treated with respect whether you are at work, in public or hanging out with friends and family.

So, how do you become more confident in dealing with bullies? Is it really just a case of 'man up' or do you always need to take action and confront the bully head-on?

A good place to begin is by asking yourself the question: How is this situation impacting my life? Is it just a minor irritation or is it something big that is consuming your every thought and keeping you up at night? The answer you give to this question will give you a clear indicator of whether you may need to learn to detach or ignore the situation, or whether you need to take further assertive action to resolve the issue.

Although I am not encouraging you to ever simply accept poor behaviour from other people, there may be times — such as if the situation is just a little bit annoying — that the best thing you can do for your own emotional wellbeing is to choose not to engage with the other person's behaviour and, as much as possible, ignore it. People often get confused when I explain this theory, feeling that it is just a passive response that 'lets the bully off the hook'. In fact, nothing could be further from the truth. It is actually really powerful to make a conscious decision not to allow another person's bad behaviour to impact your own personal happiness and wellbeing. When you do this, you are coming from a place of empowerment and confidence and choosing to take back your power from them.

In doing this, you send out a clear message that you are not going to allow another person's crappy behaviour to get in the way of you feeling good. This is also a great act of self-care. Therefore, on some occasions, the best strategy for dealing with a bully might be to just be a little bit more conscious and mindful in the way you choose to react to them.

I do admit that sometimes this is more easily said than done, particularly if feelings of hurt and resentment have been building up for a while. It is at times like these that detaching may feel most difficult. We will learn how to deal with these types of situations further on in this chapter.

MINDSET

Let's start with mindset. Remember, as a human being you always have a choice on how you perceive or react to any given situation. You can choose to look at yourself as a victim, continuing to allow those 'why me' thoughts to race through your head, or you can choose to stand back, take a few deep breaths and reclaim your power. Yes, you may feel that you have every right to feel angry and resentful, but ultimately, if you choose the victim path you will only end up feeling even more helpless and powerless.

The more powerful and empowering approach is to take the time to ask yourself the following questions:

- **What do I need to do to feel better about this situation and take back my power from this person?**

- **How do I need to react to this situation to make myself feel better?**

By doing this, you give space for your mind to create endless possibilities of what you need to do in order to take back your power and step away from being a victim of bullying. Not only will your answers to these questions provide you with new choices and actions, but they will also leave you feeling more in control of your life.

JODY

Jody was becoming annoyed with her mother-in-law always giving unwanted advice about how she thought Jody should bring up her children. Overall, Jody had a good relationship with her mother-in-law but was finding that these criticisms were really getting on her nerves and she was starting to resent her mother-in-law's presence.

Jody admitted that although she found her mother-in-law's behaviour irritating, it wasn't something that was keeping her up at night — even if she did find it rather annoying at the time! Therefore she decided the best course of action for her to take was to reclaim her power and choose not to allow the comments to

upset her any further. As a result, the next time her mother-in-law threw a comment her way relating to Jody's parenting techniques, Jody simply took a deep breath, put her best smile on her face and replied, 'Oh, thanks for your opinion, it's interesting that you see things that way.' After another comment, she was able to respond with, 'Oh, that's fascinating.'

The good news is that after practising these responses over a few days, Jody realized that her mother-in-law's comments no longer irritated her, and any feelings of resentment had simply dissipated. In fact, Jody would just end up smiling on the inside, recognizing that she had taken her power back from her mother-in-law and that she was no longer allowing her mother-in-law's behaviour to irritate her.

There are many occasions when it is a good strategy to make a choice to react in a new and different way to minor irritations; however, as mentioned earlier, things can get a little more complicated when more serious issues are involved — in particular, this includes any incident that makes you feel threatened, scared, upset or depressed. If your emotional wellbeing is suffering, this is usually a sign that you not only need to take your power back in your mind, but you also need to take some action to protect yourself.

In these more serious situations, start by evaluating the relationship with the person concerned. Is this someone you really need to spend time with? Do you need to be around them at all? If it is a friend or family member, evaluate the relationship you have with them and see how necessary it is for you to spend time with them. Is it really in your best interests to have a friendship or relationship with them, going forward? If it is a romantic relationship that you are in, then you really should not be tolerating any type of bullying or toxic behaviour.

It may sound simple, but one of the easiest ways to take back your power and stop bullying behaviour is to choose to put some distance between the two of you and stop engaging with each other.

Unfortunately, there are situations where you may find yourself having regular contact with a bully, such as at work or when dealing with a close member of your family. In these cases, it is key to put a plan in place and look at what needs to happen in order for you to take your power back and feel safe and respected. Although this path may feel a little scary, remind yourself of what your life will be like if you choose to do nothing. Do you really think anything is likely to change if you don't take action? Probably not, so just how long are you willing to put up with this situation?

The following is a list of suggested actions you could take:

- **Tell someone you trust what has been happening. This might be a colleague or supervisor at work (if it's a work bullying situation) or a relative or friend (if it's a family bullying situation). You may also want to speak with your doctor if you feel the situation is impacting your physical and/or mental wellbeing.**

- **If it is workplace bullying, speak with another manager, the union or the human-resources department.**

- **Gain support or advice from a support service or government agency in your local area. Support groups are available in most countries, so please do reach out for a trained counsellor if you need expert help.**

- **If you feel it is necessary, document what is going on. Who was there? What happened? How did you feel? Writing things down can help you gain clarity and also leverage if you need to report or take further action against the bully.**

- Take some reflection time to get clear on what assertive conversation you would like to have. Write it down if it helps.

- Build up your positive self-talk and mindset before you enter into any dialogue with the person concerned.

- Consider taking a trusted friend or colleague with you for moral support when you speak to the person concerned.

- Use assertive language and clearly describe the behaviour you see the bully exhibiting. Make sure you let them know how their behaviour is impacting you. (This is often a good option with family members.)

- Always make your safety and wellbeing a priority.

Each situation will be different and there are many actions you can choose to take. What you will find is that even making a decision to do something about it and take action will boost your confidence and assist you in taking back your power from the bully.

ROBERT

CASE STUDY

Robert was being bullied by his manager at work. This included humiliating Robert in front of his work colleagues and excluding him from normal work-place activities such as team meetings. Robert dreaded going to work each day and often felt angry and frustrated. He was also having trouble sleeping and was becoming short-tempered with his family.

Robert looked at what he needed to do in order to take back his power and resolve the situation. He didn't feel comfortable speaking directly to his manager, so he decided to seek support from his

organization's human-resources department. In addition, he also spoke to an outside association that offered support and advice in dealing with workplace bullying.

Importantly, Robert also took responsibility for his own emotional wellbeing by going for a walk over lunch each day. This helped him to relieve stress and feel in control of the situation.

ASSERTIVENESS AROUND BULLIES

Whatever action you decide is right for you, remember to be as assertive as possible. Re-read the chapter on assertive skills (see page 74) and also support yourself with assertive words and body language, which includes standing up straight and looking the person directly in the eye. Prepare in advance by practising your assertiveness statements in front of the mirror and use the broken-record technique (see page 83) if required.

Good assertive statements to use with bullies include:

- **I've recently noticed signs that you are trying to bully me and I want this behaviour to stop.**

- **I would like you to stop behaving like that.**

- **Stop doing that now!**

- **I feel offended by your remark.**

- **I would like you to respect my point of view.**

In summary, when dealing with any kind of toxic behaviour, it is likely that your confidence will take a hit. You may even blame yourself or start to believe comments or unkind words that the bully may throw at you. You may even start to believe deep down that you deserve their cruel or unreasonable behaviour. A word of warning on this — don't even go there! If you start down this path you will be internally bullying yourself with similar thoughts and criticism.

During any type of stressful situation where your confidence may have taken a hit, it is imperative that you focus your energy back on yourself; be kind to, and nurture yourself with soothing words. Keep reminding yourself that you did not bring this situation on yourself, nor are you responsible in any way. If you have taken appropriate action, concentrate on the positives in doing this — you actually care enough about yourself to take back your power! Remember, you always have a choice and at any moment you can choose to torment yourself or you can choose to walk away with your head held high knowing you have taken steps to look after your wellbeing.

I also recommend that you go back and work on a few more of the steps in Chapter 13, 'What do you like about you?'. These simple steps will assist you in building up that confidence muscle so that looking after your own emotional wellbeing becomes a priority for you, regardless of the situation you may find yourself in.

TIPS FOR CONFIDENCE WITH BULLIES

- **Take extra care of yourself at this time. Surround yourself with nurturing people and get adequate exercise, food and rest.**

- **Give up the need to think that there is anything you can say or do to make the bully be nice to you.**

- **Remember that any bullying situation is not about you. The bully is the one with the problem, not you.**

- **Be clear that some people are toxic and there is nothing you can do to change them. You do, however, need to learn to protect yourself.**

- **It is okay to release people from your life who are not supportive and kind.**

- **It is acceptable to walk away from someone if they continually make you unhappy.**

CHAPTER 16

CONFIDENCE IN YOUR CAREER

Feeling and looking confident in your chosen career can actually be more important than your qualifications, skills or experience. Research shows that those who appear more confident at work not only receive more respect from their employers but are more likely to be offered the best career opportunities.

Let's be honest: if you don't have self-belief and confidence in your own career, why should anyone else? The truth is that if you continually doubt your own ability, these doubts will manifest as unconscious messages or 'vibes' that your body sends out. These messages are then communicated to, and felt by, the people around you. Therefore, if you are sending out vibes such as 'I don't believe in myself, so neither should you,' or 'I feel insecure in my career,' you may just find yourself overlooked at work for promotion opportunities and further career advancement. In addition, you may also be self-sabotaging your career progress by not taking the risk of stepping forward because deep down you believe that you are not going to succeed anyway.

This chapter will focus on two key areas. We will begin by looking at the importance of confidence both before and during the interview process and then follow on with steps you can take to assist you in feeling confident within your career.

CONFIDENT INTERVIEWS

If you find a job that interests you and for which you are keen to apply, how can you set yourself up for success to ensure you get that all-important interview?

The first key step is to get that resume up to date. Yes, I am sure you are aware of the importance of a good resume, but when was the last time you reviewed yours in detail to make sure it reflected your current skills and achievements?

There are three key reasons for a good resume:

- **To introduce yourself to a future employer.**

- **To promote your knowledge, skills and accomplishments.**

- **To successfully obtain an interview.**

Your resume is the first impression a future employer has from you, so it needs to be as impressive as possible. If you have been out of work for a while, or writing and grammar are not really your strengths, then support yourself by getting some expert help to write your resume.

The content of your resume must always be concise, succinct and to the point. Poor spelling, grammar and punctuation are a huge put-off to a prospective employer, so take the time to get these right. Let's face it, why should an organization take the time to interview you if you couldn't be bothered running your resume through a spell check?

As a final tip, always ensure that all the information contained in your resume is factual. I know that it's tempting to embellish your experience or qualifications in order to impress, but my advice is to always stick to the truth. Being honest in your resume will help you feel more confident because you will be answering questions during interviews based on accurate information about your qualifications and employment history.

Confidence in interviews

Being confident during the interview process can also set you apart when you are up against other suitably qualified candidates. Don't underestimate the importance of good body language. Your resume may be impressive but if your body language or demeanour is filled with uncertainty and doubt, then the interviewer will pick up on it.

I highly recommend that you take the time to visualize yourself having a great interview experience. You could imagine yourself walking confidently into the interview room and sitting down feeling comfortable and relaxed. Then continue to see yourself answering any questions effortlessly. Finally, as the interview comes to a close, picture yourself walking out the interview room feeling fabulous and happy, confident that you have got the job.

As with anything we have discussed in this book, a positive and encouraging mindset is key. Don't focus on what could go wrong during the interview; focus on what could go right. Try not to allow any past experiences or old irrational beliefs scare you about the interview process, such as worrying that you won't be able to answer the questions perfectly or fearing that you may end up saying something stupid.

If you do find yourself feeling anxious or doubtful prior to an interview, take the time to calm yourself by using soothing and encouraging words.

Try some of these soothing phrases for a start:

- **It will be okay; it is perfectly normal for me to feel nervous.**

- **I did well to even get the interview, so I can only try my best from here.**

- **I will be able to cope with it; after all, it isn't an interrogation, and I just need to prepare well before the date comes around.**

- **This is good practice for me — the more I do interviews, the more confident I will feel.**

- **Hey, what is the worst that can happen? The job may not be ideal for me anyway!**

The last point is interesting. Think about it: what if you did give yourself permission to fail at the interview? I know this sounds crazy, but if not getting this job is the worst that could really happen, then it is not exactly life-threatening, is it?

Interestingly, I have found that when people do give themselves permission to fail, they actually relax more during the interview process and end up coming across more confident and natural, rather than when they try too hard to be perfect.

Preparation

Insecurity and fear often come from feelings of not being organized or prepared, so if you want to ensure that you feel more confident during the interview, you need to invest sufficient time and energy into preparing well.

Begin by doing extensive research on the company you are interviewing for and ensure that you know about the organization's values and structure. Also set yourself up for success by researching common interview questions and practise answering some of these in the mirror or with a friend. Remember, the more you practise, the more familiar you will become with answering questions and you will be able to give more confident answers. This may also help your voice shake less during the interview!

Finally, don't be afraid to take some notes into the interview if you feel it will support you. However, try to avoid just reading from these notes like a script, and aim to memorize any important information.

Prior to the interview, a great way to give your confidence a boost is to take a few minutes to write down all the skills and traits you will bring to the job that is being offered.

Sometimes, you can get so focused on doing the 'right' thing during a job interview, that you forget that you have a great skill set to offer the employer. Remember, an interview is about exploring the possibility of making a mutually beneficial exchange, so remember to value yourself and the unique knowledge, skills and resources that you can bring to the table. Don't forget to prepare a few good questions for the employer as well, so you can work out if the job on offer is really a good fit for you.

On the day of the interview

If you have prepared well, worked on building up a confident mindset and are clear on the knowledge and skills you can offer, you are already on your way to being a great interviewee. Don't forget to give yourself a few well-deserved words of praise, and remind yourself that you wouldn't have been invited along to the interview if you were not already being considered for the job.

Here are a few more additional tips to boost your interview confidence:

- Always allow extra time to get to the interview. Being late or rushing around trying to find the location of the interview will create unwanted stress and leave you feeling flustered and anxious even before the interview starts.

- While waiting to be called in for interview, take a few minutes to ground yourself through a few slow, steady, deep breaths; this will help you to relax and calm your mind.

- Act with confidence. Be aware of your body language and think about your posture. Stand up straight with your shoulders back and move with confidence and purpose. Shake hands confidently.

- Maintain eye contact throughout the interview. This gives the impression you are engaged and interested. If you are being interviewed by several people, make sure you share your eye contact between all attendees. If you have your resume in front of you on a desk, feel free to rest your eyes by taking a brief glimpse at it.

- If you need some time to answer a question or your mind goes blank, empower yourself by taking a pause and requesting that the interviewer either repeat the question or explain the question more clearly. Don't put yourself under pressure to answer questions quickly, because you may just end up confusing yourself and mixing up your words. Take your time and answer each question calmly and clearly.

- Remind yourself that the interviewer is also human and is probably nervous as well. Don't let your mind trick you into

thinking of the interviewer as someone who is intimidating or that they are trying to catch you out in some way.

- **You don't have to be perfect. Just do your best.**

When it's over

Once the interview is over, it's time to give yourself some well-deserved praise and encouragement. Don't get hung up focusing on any parts of the interview you feel didn't go as well as expected — this will just eat away at your confidence. To ensure you keeping building your confidence muscle, it is therefore preferable to focus on at least two areas of the interview that you felt went well rather than lingering on any perceived mistakes or shortfalls in your interview technique. Remember, you are not a mind reader, so you have no idea what impression you made on the interviewer. Build yourself up by focusing on the things that went well in the interview rather than what you feel could have worked better.

Waiting to hear from a potential employer can also be nerve-racking, so don't fall into the trap of assuming the worst. If you haven't heard anything by the anticipated decision date, rather than sitting around feeling anxious, choose to empower yourself by sending a short, polite email reaffirming your interest. If you prefer to call, I recommend doing this after a week. Always remain professional and don't keep hassling the organization for answers. They may just be taking their time or even waiting for the job budget to be approved.

If you do get offered the job, well done! However, it is just as important to give yourself a well-deserved pat on the back even if you were not successful for this position. Don't allow thoughts such as 'I wasn't good enough' or 'I have failed' to flood your mind. Remember not to make circumstances mean something negative about yourself or jump to unsubstantiated conclusions. This will do nothing apart from make you feel down on yourself and eat away at your confidence.

It is far more beneficial for your confidence to encourage yourself with thoughts such as:

- **That was great interview practice for when the right job comes along.**

- **I now feel more confident going for interviews.**

- **This was all part of my journey towards a great new role.**

CONFIDENCE ON THE JOB

Take a few minutes to reflect on the job or career that you are currently in — does it make you happy and do you enjoy it? If your answer is a cut-and-dried 'no' and as a result you have to drag yourself out of bed each morning, it may be time to think about a career change. We spend around 90,000 hours at work in an average lifetime, and if you hate your job, each and every one of these hours you spend at work might be robbing you of your happiness and your health.

According to a Gallup Poll, over 80 per cent of people dislike their job — if this resonates with you, it may be time to take back your power and find a job that makes you feel happy. I know that this may not be a simple prospect for many people, but remember that you can make your career change gradually in small, comfortable steps, rather than taking a huge leap into the unknown.

When you do work in a job that you enjoy, you will bring your best to work each morning and feel good about it. When you feel like this on a regular basis, life just naturally works better and your confidence muscle will become stronger and vibrant. So, explore other opportunities if you need to — life is really too short to hate your work.

Clients who come to me for help in their career often feel stuck, unmotivated or bored. Others feel stressed, unappreciated or find it difficult to create that all-important work–life balance. What the majority of these clients have in common is that they are just simply waiting around for their situation to improve, a better opportunity to come along or maybe a promotion or pay increase to land on their lap. As a result, they are in limbo just hoping someone or something will come along to magically resolve their issues or make things better for them.

This approach merely renders you powerless. As with any situation in life, you alone are responsible for your life, happiness and career. Therefore, if you don't like what is happening, you can make the choice today to take back your power and do something about it.

Be honest with yourself: how long are you going to wait around for your career to improve or for you to feel better at work? Days? Months? Years?

TOP TIPS TO TAKE BACK YOUR POWER IN YOUR CAREER

- **Make time, at least once a year, to evaluate your career satisfaction, direction and progress. Are you happy with what you do? Are you heading in the right direction?**

- **Are you enjoying your work? Are there parts of your job you would like to do more or less of? Do you need to organize a meeting with your manager to discuss? Remember, if you don't ask — you won't get!**

- **Set a goal for your career. Are you on track? Do you need to change anything? Is your goal still relevant or do you need to update it? Does it still feel good to you? What do you need to do in order to head in the direction of your goal?**

- **Make the most of annual reviews, and ask for feedback. If you are looking for further opportunities in the** organization, make this clear to your manager and also let them know your future career goals.

- **Suggest improvements. If there are problems in your role, don't just complain about it, take responsibility and suggest solutions. You won't know until you try.**

- **Focus on the positives. Even if you dislike your job immensely, there must be some positives in it somewhere. Does it enable you to travel?, pay the bills or allow you good work–life balance? Sometimes just a little mindset change is required for you to feel more positive about your job.**

- **Do you need to start looking for another job that will satisfy you more and is more aligned to your values, passions and strengths?**

- **Get external help. Do you need to get yourself a career coach who will support you to find your passion in life or start your own business?**

JOHN

CASE STUDY

John was unhappy in his role at work. He had been doing the same job for several years and was starting to get bored and also feel a little unappreciated. He enjoyed the company culture and didn't want to leave but was unsure what to do next in order to feel happier in his career.

John had fallen into the trap of waiting for something to happen to make him feel better in his job. I reminded John that he had access to his own personal power and if he wanted things to improve, it was up to him to do something about it! Therefore, during our coaching session, John explored the different options he could take in order to take his power back in his career. These included:

- Speaking to his manager about his interest in expanding his role and learning new skills.
- Speaking to other managers within the organization about the possibility of taking on a secondment in a new area.
- Looking into taking an external course that interested him.
- Making a decision that, in the absence of positive feedback at work, John would start to give himself some well-deserved praise instead.
- Although John wasn't planning on leaving the company, he also investigated similar roles in other organizations.

A few months later John reported that he was feeling far more motivated and happy at work. The simple action of praising himself had led to him feeling proud of all his accomplishments and he was enjoying the new tasks and challenges that his manager had agreed to give him. An added bonus was that John's manager was really impressed by his willingness to stand up and ask for what he wanted!

Speaking up in meetings

It is common to feel nervous about speaking up during workplace meetings. Some people are simply more introverted and prefer to listen carefully instead of joining in. That is perfectly fine and I am a big believer in being true to your own personality, but what can you do when you desperately wish to play a more active role in meetings, get more involved and speak your mind with confidence and ease?

Many people are hesitant about speaking up during meetings because they fear they may say the wrong thing and be judged negatively by the people around them. Many also stay quiet through the fear that they have little to contribute.

CASE STUDY

STACEY

Stacey felt lacking in confidence at work. She had recently attended a team meeting where her manager asked the team to come up with a solution to a problem they were experiencing. Even though Stacey felt she had the perfect solution, she didn't say a word because she was worried that people would laugh at her idea. A few minutes later, another member of her team spoke up and suggested the very same thing that Stacey had been thinking about, and everyone was really impressed. As a result, Stacey felt annoyed and frustrated at herself for keeping quiet and not having the confidence to share what had been her prized answer all along.

TOP TIPS FOR CONFIDENCE DURING MEETINGS

- Remind yourself that you have the job you are in because your employer believes you are valuable, have expert skills and something to contribute.

- Create a mindset of safety and ask yourself what really is the worst that could happen.

- Value your ideas. Remind yourself that you are a valuable person and are just as likely as anyone else to come up with good ideas.

- If you sit in meetings worrying about speaking up, you will just find it harder to enter a discussion. Try taking back your power and choosing to be one of the first people to speak within ten minutes of the opening of the meeting. Start by just agreeing with another person, or discussing something that happened in the past. This will help build up your confidence muscle and release any fears that people are judging you.

- **Don't censor yourself. If an idea comes up in your head, don't let it sit around attracting self-doubt. Bite the bullet and speak up. The more you do this, the more confident you will feel in entering into any discussion. Don't forget to praise yourself afterwards.**

ACTION STEP

Make a commitment to yourself to speak up at your next work meeting. If possible, review the agenda and choose a topic ahead of time. This will prepare you in advance to contribute to the discussion.

Asking for what you want

We spend a lot of time at work, so it is not a surprise that problems and issues raise their ugly head. These could include frustration with our manager and co-workers or topics such as workload, rate of pay or promotion prospects.

In an ideal world, employees should be able to discuss issues openly and safely. However, the reality is that many workers feel afraid to speak up and voice their concerns at work, particularly to someone in authority or a person who is higher up the organizational chain. Indeed, according to management researchers Kathleen Ryan and Daniel Oestreich, 70 per cent of the people they studied from various industries and job titles were afraid to speak up at work for fear of repercussions.

Many employees often make a choice to keep quiet in order to avoid any possible backlash. This is particularly true if they have financial and family commitments and feel there might be a risk to their job or livelihood.

I believe that, despite the perceived risks, speaking up and asking for what you want is a vital and important skill to practise in life. Not only does it often result in you actually getting what you want, but speaking up can also help resolve difficult situations and improve your working environment. People who speak up regularly are rated far more highly by their bosses than those who keep quiet.

I have seen, time and time again, cases where choosing not to speak up just leads to increased resentment and stress, which often spills over to personal and family life.

We often feel resentment when we are under the impression that an individual, group or even organization has hurt or wronged us in some way. These feelings can come from a variety of situations including a lack of promotion or recognition, feeling overworked, jealousy of a colleague or simply the lack of financial recognition for the job that is being done.

Therefore, it is often in the best interests of our careers and our health to learn how to have those awkward workplace conversations. Although this might not sound like a comfortable option, how are you ever going to get what you truly want and deserve if you don't learn how to ask for it? Remember, people are not mind readers! Let's face it, even if you don't ultimately end up getting what you want, you will still find yourself in a much better position to work out what you need to do next, and you will have the added bonus of feeling empowered that you even had the conversation in the first place.

When you choose to speak up, you send out a message that you are taking responsibility for your own needs and wants. So, whether it is requesting to work alternative hours, take a holiday, ask for greater resources or create improved work–life balance, it is a far better approach to bite the bullet and state, 'This is what I would like, why I want it and these are the reasons you should give it to me,' than to sit around feeling resentful and pointing the blame finger at other people for the situation you find yourself in.

I do recognize that whether it is down to the fear of repercussion or just a general avoidance of any difficult conversations, speaking up at work does not always come easily. Many of us are taught from a very early age to be polite and never challenge or ask for help from people in authority, and this can pose extra challenges for our confidence muscle. However, make sure you remind yourself that you deserve to value and honour your own needs, and this includes asking for help and support. It also sends out a strong message to your employer that you value yourself and are keen to offer opinions and make suggestions for improvement.

If you are still in doubt or feeling anxious about the benefits of speaking up, ask yourself what will happen if you allow things to continue the way they are and nothing changes. What will be the outcome? Will you continue to feel resentful and carry around these toxic thoughts and feelings? Will you end up just taking more sick days? How will this help your career? When answering these questions, most people realize that there are more upsides to speaking up than doing nothing and keeping quiet.

Try these steps to build up your confidence muscle when speaking up at work:

- **Remind yourself of your Personal Bill of Rights (see page 34) and relate these rights to your working environment.**

- **Boost your mindset by encouraging yourself and reminding yourself of the benefit of asking for what you want.**

- **Set yourself up with a mindset of safety.**

- **Don't be afraid of conflict; it is a normal part of life to disagree. Try not to get defensive or take things personally. Listen to what is being said and build on areas of agreement.**

- **Prepare well — don't be afraid to take in supporting documentation if you need to.**

- **Schedule a meeting in advance in your boss's diary to discuss your concerns.**

- **Don't go into a meeting feeling resentful and angry. If you feel like this, take a few minutes to write down how you are feeling, and your concerns, in a journal before going into the meeting. Only go into the meeting when you feel calm.**

- **Be assertive and avoid aggression. Look for a win–win situation and offer suggestions for how things can be improved.**

- **Be clear on the outcome you would like and use assertive statements beginning with 'I' such as 'I would like to discuss my performance rating with you,' or 'I would like to take this opportunity to discuss my pay rise.' (See also Chapter 11 for more tips.) Avoid using blame statements such as 'You did this,' or 'John in the office is annoying me.'**

- **Be okay with saying 'no'. Don't get into the habit of thinking that you will not progress in your career or gain people's respect if you turn down requests. The opposite is actually true — nobody likes a doormat, and if you are one of those people who is too agreeable, then the chances are that you will just get extra work piled on and may be overlooked for promotion.**

Do you doubt your abilities?

When we feel confident at work, we tend to make better decisions, be more assertive and take greater initiative. We also feel less stressed and have a raised sense of accomplishment and contribution.

Doubting your abilities, believing that a co-worker is better than you or not believing you can do a good enough job are common examples of low self-confidence in your career. This might lead to feelings of helplessness and increased anxiety and stress levels. In the long run, there is little doubt that these feelings can ultimately affect your work and career success.

The opposite of self-doubt is self-efficacy: the belief in your own skills and abilities to complete tasks and achieve goals. Although it is perfectly normal sometimes to doubt your abilities, continuing to buy into the voices of doom will drag you down and undermine your performance and career confidence.

When this voice of doom in your head sounds more limiting than supportive, it is time to take control and challenge these old thought patterns.

It is key to first accept that you feel the way that you do but also recognize that you are not powerless to change things. Remember, you always have a choice to reclaim or give away your power, whether to a person or an old thought pattern that no longer serves you. Learn to recognize which situations trigger these thoughts and your self-doubt, and do something to resolve it. For example, if a lack of skills in a particular area makes you doubt your ability, go ahead and empower yourself by getting the training you need or asking for additional support.

A helpful exercise I use in my coaching practice is to transform self-doubting thoughts into more realistic and supportive statements. For example, if you find yourself thinking 'I won't be able to do this,' replace this thought with 'I will give this a try and do my best.' Or instead of telling yourself that a task is 'too difficult for me', replace this thought with a more encouraging statement such as 'The more I give it a go, the more I will learn how to do this.' These kinder thoughts will give you some additional breathing space and help you ease the need to beat yourself up.

If you find yourself doing a new task for the first time and doubt your ability, remind yourself that it is perfectly normal to feel apprehensive. Remember, everyone learns at different speeds, so don't give yourself a hard time if you don't pick up a new task immediately. Once your brain gets the hang of it, you will be on a roll!

Also try these affirmations for releasing self-doubt:

- **I am really looking forward to feeling more confident in my career.**

- **I will be fine; it is natural to be better at some things than others, and I will just keep trying my best.**

- **It doesn't matter if I make a mistake; it is part of the learning process.**

- **Although it doesn't feel like it right now, I am sure I will work it out.**

> **'I always used to panic when I felt I didn't know how to do a task I had been asked to do. Until I realized that this was normal — now I just take my time, encourage myself and ask for help from others if I need it.' Shelly, 32**

Another useful way to build up your confidence muscle at work is to focus on your existing strengths, rather than your perceived weaknesses. Take the time to make a list of all your achievements and things you feel good about in your career. Keep this list close by to help you to remember the great things you have done and also give you a confidence boost when you most need it.

Finally, please don't fall into the trap of comparing your achievements to those of your work colleagues. I admit, when I was starting my coaching practice I nearly drove myself mad comparing myself to the achievements of other coaches around me. Fortunately, this stopped when I reminded myself that everyone has different skills and abilities and I had my own unique set of talents. So, take a leaf out of my book and quit comparing yourself to other people and instead, celebrate your own accomplishments!

ACTION STEP

Keep a record of your achievements and completed projects. This information is useful to remind yourself of all the great work you have done so far. It is also a useful list to have to hand during your performance reviews and when updating your resume.

TOP TIPS TO BUILD CAREER CONFIDENCE

- Choose a career that you enjoy and that matches your values and passions.

- Learn from your career mistakes and then move on. Making mistakes is part of the learning process and nobody ever gets anywhere without making a few mistakes along the way.

- Don't allow other people's negative comments to get you down. Remember, you know yourself better than anyone else does, so don't let outside points of view influence your opinion of yourself — that goes for your manager as well!

- Change your mindset from thinking 'I can't do something,' to 'I can't do something yet.'

- Don't just hide at your desk: speak to your work colleagues, build empathy skills and find a common ground from which to start conversations.

- Write a career goal and visualize yourself feeling happy and confident in your career.

- Don't be afraid to put yourself forward for career opportunities — what do you have to lose?

- Replace fear with faith. Commit to doing one thing a week that scares you. This could be trying something new, making a presentation to other people or attending a networking event. Don't forget to use your thoughts to encourage you and soothe your fears.

- Don't try to become a mind reader believing that people see you in a certain way at work. Are you making things mean something negative about yourself without examining the factual evidence?

CHAPTER 17

CONFIDENCE IN RELATIONSHIPS

I don't think there is another area that tests our confidence as much as our romantic relationships. It doesn't matter whether you are looking for a partner, currently in a relationship or even looking to end one: confidence is key.

Many of us struggle to find that relationship we truly desire. We may feel deep down that there is something wrong with us if we are single for a long time or haven't yet settled down with that ideal mate. We look wishfully at other couples, wondering if and when the time will ever come for us to find love. When we do find a relationship, we find ourselves worrying that the other person might not hang around, or turning ourselves inside out trying to be the perfect partner. We might also end up staying in a relationship longer than is healthy for us because we fear being alone.

I get it — some people make the entire relationship process look effortlessly natural, while some of us struggle to even get a date. So, what can we do in order to feel more confident about our relationships?

The beliefs we have about ourselves and the thoughts that accompany them play a huge part in whether our relationships are few and far between, toxic or healthy and nourishing. If deep down we truly believe we have much to offer a partner and see ourselves as a great catch, then our relationships will reflect this. We will refuse to settle for anything less than the best and be less likely to lose ourselves in relationships.

However, if our thoughts are filled with negative messages such as, 'It will be difficult for me to find the partner I want,' or 'People don't seem interested in having a relationship with me,' then the quality of our relationships will also reflect this.

> **'I never thought I was attractive enough to find a relationship. As a result I always hid in the kitchen at parties and never really tried to start a conversation with a person I was attracted to. I just didn't think they would be interested in me.' Emma, 27**

Let's dig in a little deeper and explore relationship beliefs by comparing them to the working of a photocopy machine. Yes, you heard me right, a photocopy machine.

Whenever you feed a sheet of paper into a photocopier, you get a mirror image, a copy, out the other side — correct? Now, this may sound rather strange, but this is precisely the same way life and relationships work. Simply put, whatever beliefs you hold about yourself and your relationships, whether or not you are aware of them, get fed into the photocopier of life and are then copied and shown to you as output in the different parts of your life. For example, if you hold a belief that it will be difficult to find a partner, then in reality, you will find it difficult to meet a partner.

Let me explain this in more detail. When you hold a negative belief (consciously or unconsciously) such as 'I am unlovable' or 'I don't deserve love', this belief is copied back to you in the form of only meeting people who are incapable of loving you. This might mean that you only attract unavailable or toxic partners.

Likewise, if you believe that you are unworthy of a great relationship, you might attract people in your life who treat you badly or have little respect for you. If you believe that you have missed the boat and will not be able to find a partner, then you might find yourself meeting only people who are married or otherwise unavailable for relationships.

A great way to examine the beliefs that are currently working in your own personal photocopier of life is to look at patterns you are experiencing in your relationships. For example, if you have found it difficult in the past to meet anyone or get a date, you might be holding on to a negative belief that people are not interested in you or that you will find it difficult to meet anyone nice. If you find that your relationships are always short term, you could have a negative belief that relationships never last or people always leave you.

Other common negative relationship beliefs include:

- **I am too old to meet someone.**

- **Other people find it much easier than I do to find relationships.**

- **I am just not cut out for relationships.**

- **Other people are far more attractive than I am.**

- **Other people just have more luck than I do with relationships.**

- **As soon as I get to know someone, they lose interest.**

- **It is difficult to meet anyone.**

- **There are no good men/women around.**

There are literally thousands of different negative beliefs that can impact relationships, but the important thing is to remember that these are simply old programs that are repeated over and over again. This is why we find ourselves re-living similar experiences — wanted or unwanted!

ACTION STEP

Take some time out to examine your beliefs about your personal relationships. If they are positive and feel good to you, then keep hold of them. However, if they are negative and are restricting you from living the life you truly desire, it is time to do some work on feeding some new beliefs into your photocopier of life.

The good news is that regardless of the relationship beliefs you hold, you can choose to learn to override them by consciously amending what is being fed into your photocopier of life. In doing this, you create new 'copies' or beliefs, which of course lead to new, improved relationship experiences. One of the ways you can do this is by consciously choosing to program your mind (and photocopier) with thoughts and beliefs that nurture you and ensure that you only attract healthy and nourishing relationships.

As I discussed earlier in this book, your negative relationship beliefs are just old spam and programming, much of which was not yours to begin with. Remember, you soaked up the majority of this programming when you were only a child and it is not only meaningless, it is simply untrue.

As an adult, you can now choose to take responsibility for your future relationships and let this old programming go. Many of us have identified with this outdated programming for so long that it has become our identity, but I promise you, it is never too late to change things. Think about it: the only reason you have not been having the relationship that you desire is that you have been feeding the same old belief pattern into the photocopier for most of your life. It is now the perfect time for you to take back your power from this old programming. Whatever you put into your photocopier you get out as a mirror image, so can you imagine how different your life is going to be when you start to put some delicious new thoughts about relationships into the input tray?

In the affirmations chapter (see page 86), I pointed out the importance of choosing a few affirmations or conscious thoughts that can help re-program your mind and create new neural pathways. We are now going to use this method again, focusing specifically on relationships.

To make this process as effective as possible, we again need to start with an affirmation that feels good to you and doesn't cause you to doubt it or feel anxious about how or when it is going to happen. Try to tune into your body while you are doing this, and if you feel that an affirmation brings up any type of doubt inside you, go back and try another one that feels more comfortable and believable. This is usually the one that feels good and makes you smile!

Start with a general affirmation and just use this until you get bored with it. Then move on to choose another one when you are ready.

Try starting with:

- **It is safe for me to start thinking more positively about my relationships.**

- **It is easy for me to create new positive beliefs about my relationships.**

- **I am starting to believe that it is possible for me to have the relationship that I desire.**

- **I would really love to feel more positive about my relationships.**

- **It's great that I am beginning to change my attitude about relationships.**

- **Wouldn't it be nice if I could go on a great date?**

- **It is going to feel really good when I start dating really nice people.**

- **I am really looking forward to the time when I enjoy relationships.**

- **I can and I am improving my experience of relationships.**

- **I trust myself to be able to handle a relationship. I am safe!**

- **My perfect partner is being drawn to me now.**

- **I can create new relationship experiences.**

The good news is that these affirmations will start to program your mind with what is possible for your relationships, rather than just running on the outdated programming. Every time you practise the affirmations and they feel good to you, you are creating new positive programming that leads to new positive experiences. Just repeat your affirmations out loud or in your head at least ten times a day — more if you like, but always make sure that they feel good to you.

SAM

CASE STUDY

Sam was fed up with all his relationships being short term. It seemed that he no sooner got to know someone over a few months than they were telling him the relationship was over and he was back to being single again. A similar pattern had happened three times over the past few years.

In listening to Sam's relationship history, I could tell that all he had been unconsciously feeding his life copier was beliefs such as, 'All my relationships are only short term,' or 'Relationships don't last for me.' As a result, we worked on choosing some fresh new affirmation statements that felt good to Sam. These included:

- I am looking forward to having a good long-term healthy relationship.
- Wouldn't it be great if I was in a really nice long-term committed relationship where I felt wonderful and nourished every day?
- I am a great catch — all my other past relationships have been great practice for my life partner coming into my life.

I didn't see Sam again for several years, and the good news is that he is now happily married with a family.

NEEDINESS

Now that we have started to shift some of your old outdated beliefs about relationships, let's focus on other times that you might struggle with relationship confidence.

I want to make this really clear for you from the start: feeling confident in relationships is not about your partner, it is about you.

Nothing interferes with the ability to have an authentic committed relationship as much as low confidence and poor self-esteem. So, if you are the type of person who is always looking for your partner to make you feel loved, worthy, attractive or special, then you are going about this in completely the wrong way and you will only end up in relationships that cause you frustration and heartache. This is never a reason to be hard on yourself, but it is an indication that it is time for you to focus your energy on healing yourself, rather than trying to get your partner to change their behaviour in order to make you feel good.

The reality is, you must respect yourself enough to insist on healthy relationships. If you don't have sufficient confidence in yourself or don't value who you are, the chances are that you may end up being needy in a relationship and constantly be on the lookout for any sign, signal or word that gives you some assurance that your relationship is going to be okay, and also, that you are okay.

Traits such as neediness are often associated with negative beliefs including not feeling loveable, good enough or worthy enough — beliefs that might have been carried around since childhood. They may also be associated with a shortage of trust, and a fear of rejection or abandonment.

These wounded negative beliefs are often left dormant in our mind and body until something or somebody comes along and triggers them. At this point, it is as if they take on a life of their own, rising to the surface and causing anxiety and confusion. It is common for this to happen in our relationships, because who better to show us our wounds than the person we want to accept and love us? When these wounds are triggered, we often try as hard as we can to push them down, or find something to cover them up, which gives us a feeling of relief for a short period of time. Hence when you find yourself being needy in a relationship, you are simply searching for a band-aid to cover up those old wounds.

Needy people are searching for approval and attention from other people in order to feel good and soothe their wounds. In relationships, they look to their partner's words and actions to soothe these stressful feelings, and when this doesn't happen they can become hurt, unreasonable and jealous. This cycle is toxic and doesn't feel good for anyone, especially for the person who is feeling needy.

APRIL

CASE STUDY

April found herself feeling anxious and generally wound-up every time her partner went for a night out with his friends. Despite her partner reassuring April that he could be trusted, April's mind would be filled with 'What if' thoughts and a feeling that her partner would meet someone else and leave her. As a result, she would text him throughout the evening to check up on him, and when he responded or came home early from his night out, April would immediately relax and feel better about herself. However, if her partner failed to text her back, she would fear the worst and get upset, allowing her negative thoughts to hijack her mind.

I asked April about how she felt being in a relationship with James. She admitted to me that she was scared of losing him and never felt that she was good enough for him. As a result, she lived in fear that he would leave her. Several times, she had tried to persuade James not to go out but he insisted that his once-a-month catch-up with his friends was important to him. Unfortunately, April also attached a negative meaning to James going out without her and in her mind she made it mean that he didn't love her enough to just spend time alone with her.

In this unhealthy relationship dynamic, April was unconsciously looking to James to make her feel secure, loved and good enough because deep down she didn't believe these things of herself. As a result, these beliefs were like open wounds that she was desperately seeking for James to soothe. If James did reply to any of her texts while he was enjoying a night out, or decided to cut his night short in order to spend time with April, this would provide her with a band-aid relief moment and for a short while she would feel secure, loved and good enough. However, because April had not done any internal work on healing these wounds herself, it didn't take long for them to be triggered again and thus this painful cycle of neediness continued.

In order for April to heal this pattern and become confident in her relationships, she needed to stop putting energy into controlling James's behaviour and use this energy into feeling better and healing herself. I explained to April that this is vital — if you want love, respect and a healthy relationship, then you do need to find this within yourself first.

Are you someone who drives yourself crazy every time you don't get a phone call or date or are always wondering if your partner is looking favourably at other people walking by? If so, it's time to work on your own self-image and value. Are you someone who constantly stresses about your partner meeting someone else and leaving you? If so, then your problem could be that you probably don't believe that you are good enough for them to hang around. Are you someone who always tries to control the actions of your partner? Then it is likely you have some rejection or abandonment issues that need to be healed.

Confident people recognize their value and don't need to control anybody else's behaviour in order to feel good, because they already feel good! In addition, they are satisfied with who they are already so they don't feel the need to compare themselves to other people or put themselves down.

Finding real confidence in relationships, therefore, is about developing a strong sense of value and respect for yourself. This is the type of confidence that keeps you grounded in self-respect and insists on you being treated well. It also allows you to be clear on what is and what isn't acceptable treatment and behaviour from other people in relationships, and enables you to have good physical and emotional boundaries in place. As a result, you no longer look for other people to soothe your wounds or to reassure you that you are worthy, loveable and fabulous — because you already know that this is true.

Stop and think about this for a minute: How different would your relationships be if, rather than believing those old negative beliefs about yourself, you embraced your own magical qualities and saw yourself as a great catch? What if you knew there was really nothing wrong with you and that there is someone out there who is looking for someone just like you?

Everything I have covered so far in this book, such as valuing yourself, speaking up for what you want and liking yourself, is a key foundation to healthy committed relationships. If you date without these foundations in place, you may be in for a rocky ride and constantly looking for your partner to make you feel better about yourself. Let's face it, if you don't respect yourself, why should anyone else? Seriously, there is no shortcut here — if you want the best, you need to see yourself as the best.

'When I started to value myself in relationships, people started to value me.' Emma, 45

In those stressful times when you do feel insecure and needy in a relationship, get to work on changing your all-important mindset. Remember, neediness is only an old toxic thought pattern that is doing a good job of convincing you that you are not good enough and that you need to rely on someone else in order to feel good. Ask yourself what need it is that you are hoping to have met by another person. If it is approval, learn to approve of yourself. If it is love, then work on increasing your own self-love. If you are looking for affection and attention, give it to yourself first. Never rely on someone else or something external to you to make you feel good. Give it to yourself first!

Also ensure that you empower yourself, whether you are single or currently in a relationship. Don't wait around for things to change. If you have nothing better to do than to wait for someone to call or ask you out on a date, then go out and do something for yourself instead. Take a dance class, or catch up with friends and have some fun. Don't just wait around for that relationship to complete your life — you are already complete, so have a great life regardless of your relationship status.

ACTION STEP

Write a list of all your wonderful traits and what you have to offer a partner. Read this list at least once a week so that it creates new positive programming, and start to notice these positive traits on a daily basis.

UNHEALTHY RELATIONSHIPS

Many of us have a distorted view of what a healthy relationship is. We may have been brought up around unhealthy relationships or dysfunctional families and have little knowledge of how to take care of our own needs and feelings — particularly when we are in a relationship. As a result, we may find ourselves in abusive or unhealthy relationships, tolerating all sorts of unreasonable behaviour from partners. We may also find it difficult to leave even though we know the relationship is not good for us.

Key characteristics of healthy relationships include trust, good boundaries, communication and respect. They should enhance your life and make you feel good about yourself. An unhealthy relationship, however, may include disrespectful and controlling behaviour and will usually cause stress and anxiety.

> '**I am nearly sixty years old and have suffered pain from my relationship for the past twenty-five years. I now realize that I am choosing to stay and put up with it because I don't care about myself enough to only accept positive, nurturing relationships.' Barbara, 59**

If this sounds like you, make it a priority to get support from your friends and family, as well as professional help. These types of relationship patterns are destructive and can lead to feelings of helplessness and isolation, and even to depression. Please don't fall into the trap of believing that unhealthy relationships are all that you are worth or that they are a better option than being alone.

The truth is that the longer you choose to stay in a toxic relationship, the more it will eat away at your confidence muscle.

I can't stress this strongly enough. I spent over four years in an abusive relationship and know how destructive they can be, so be honest with your own situation and care about yourself enough to get support.

ACTION STEP

- **Research the key differences between a healthy and unhealthy relationship.**

- **Challenge your beliefs and self-defeating thoughts about your value and self-worth. You are already a valuable person, so insist on being treated like one.**

- **Don't allow your fear of rejection or abandonment to keep you trapped in an unhealthy relationship.**

'There are only TWO kinds of people being abused, the ones who COMMIT to their recovery ... and the ones who don't.' Dr Annie Kaszina PhD

CONFIDENT COMMUNICATION IN RELATIONSHIPS

The way we communicate in our relationships contributes to our overall level of confidence. Communication and confidence go hand-in-hand

and are an important element in healthy and nourishing relationships.

Here are some dos and don'ts for opening up the channels of confident communications between you and your partner:

Do

- **Be honest. Share your thoughts and feelings, even if you think they may upset your partner.**

- **Speak up. Raising a specific issue or behaviour is one of the healthiest activities a couple can engage in. For example, 'When you flirt with my friends, it makes me feel that you are not considering my feelings.'**

- **Use 'I feel' statements rather than getting defensive.**

- **Take responsibility for your own feelings.**

- **Listen to your partner's point of view — don't interrupt them when they are speaking.**

Don't

- **Swallow your feelings and shy away from conflict. If your partner respects you, they will respect what you have to say.**

- **Attack your partner or use blame statements such as 'It's all your fault,' or 'You never have any time for me anymore.'**

- **Use insults or throw cheap shots at your partner.**

- **Withdraw and refuse to communicate at all. The silent treatment is not healthy.**

- **Expect your partner to be a mind reader.**

To summarize, although you may feel nervous, speaking up and clearly sharing your needs with your partner is good self-care and shows that you value yourself within the relationship. If your partner does change their behaviour, this is great. If they don't, you will still feel good that you had the courage to speak up for yourself.

Speaking up also helps keep relationships strong and happy. Relying on mind reading to get your needs fulfilled, however, will only create feelings of resentment that could lead to the demise of your relationship.

RECOGNIZE WHEN A RELATIONSHIP IS OVER

Regardless of your reasoning, ending any kind of relationship can be tough. Many of us get so caught up in an idea of what could have been rather than what is, that we end up living in a fantasy world rather than focusing on the reality of a situation. Many people choose to remain in a relationship that they know in their heart isn't right for them, often staying put due to a fear of loneliness or being left on their own. As a result, they end up settling for something less than they really want.

Hanging on to a relationship for dear life when you know deep down that the other person has moved on or has lost interest, is not good either. Ultimately, this type of situation will knock your confidence even more, so do yourself a big favour and be honest with yourself. Love yourself enough to walk away with dignity when a relationship is over, and going forward, insist on only spending time with people who want to spend time with you.

In most cases, it helps to end a relationship as soon as you make the decision; delaying the inevitable — even if you are trying to avoid hurting someone else — can make things even worse. Try to do it kindly and think about how *you* would like to be told.

On a final note, don't fall into the trap of thinking that the end of a relationship means that you have failed. In fact, the opposite is often true. Ending a relationship often takes courage and bravery and it means that you are taking care of your own needs and wants, which is always a positive thing.

ACTION STEP

Write a list of what you are looking for from a relationship. This could be honesty, trust, reliability and kindness. Love yourself enough to insist on these things and walk away if you are not getting what you really want.

TOP TIPS TO INCREASE RELATIONSHIP CONFIDENCE

- Believe in your own value. If you don't value yourself, you will attract people who don't value you.

- Never accept constant criticism or negative behaviour from your partner.

- Be yourself and develop your own interests. Time spent away from your partner with other people is healthy.

- Don't move too quickly. Talking about future plans with your partner when you have only just met them is a red flag that things are moving too fast. Take the time to get to know someone before you determine if you are compatible. Thinking about your partner and wanting to be with them 24/7 are signs that things are moving faster than may be healthy.

- Speak up clearly in your relationship — you can't blame your partner for something if they don't know about it!

- If you are in an intimate relationship that leaves you feeling unhappy, be honest with yourself. Do you need to have a courageous conversation? Do you need to remove yourself from the relationship? Always remember that it is an act of self-care to look after your feelings and needs regardless of your relationship status.

- Don't make your partner responsible for your happiness. This can be a sign of co-dependence and can lead to feelings of resentment and frustration. You alone are responsible for your happiness, so make wise choices that serve your own wellbeing and happiness.

CHAPTER 18

CONFIDENCE IN BODY IMAGE

We live in a world that is constantly sending out flawed messages about the 'perfect' body and what 'attractive' really looks like. These messages are not solely focused towards women; men are also under scrutiny to ensure that they fit the image of the 'ideal' man.

As a result, many of us have got into the habit of judging ourselves as less attractive and appealing than we really are. When we look in the mirror, we criticize our body and beat ourselves up for falling short of that 'perfect' look. We compare our looks to the images of flawlessness that appear in the media and as a result, our thoughts become focused on what is wrong with our body, rather than what is right about it. Many of us also view attractive people as being more successful or having a higher value in society than we do, convincing ourselves that our own body shape is a sign of failure.

There are many reasons for having a negative body image. These may include:

- **Society's tendency to label some body shapes as more appealing than others.**

- **Being bullied or teased about appearance during childhood.**

- **Picking up negative programming in our childhood from other people who may be unhappy with their own body shape.**

- **Being influenced by the media: TV, the press, the internet, radio and magazines.**

Each and every one of us has our own personal opinion about the way we see ourselves. Many of us are satisfied with certain parts of our body but strongly dislike other parts. Those with a negative body image may also have an excessive concern about their appearance and feel ashamed of the way they look. In some cases, this leads to depression and the development of painful eating disorders.

> **'I was at the gym seven days a week, making it my mission to increase my muscle tone so that I felt attractive.' Adam, 28**

NEGATIVE BODY IMAGE VERSUS POSITIVE BODY IMAGE

You may have a negative body image if you experience the following:

- **You feel ashamed, awkward and uncomfortable in your body.**

- **You place greater value on how you look on the outside than the person you are on the inside.**

- **You compare yourself unfavourably to other people.**

- **You find it difficult to accept compliments about the way you look.**

- **You wish your life away believing that you will only find happiness once you improve your body shape or lose any excess weight.**

If you hate, criticize or feel ashamed of your body, you are never going to feel particularly good about yourself. Negative body image is not only bad for your health, it is also incredibly time-consuming and a waste of your precious energy. It prevents you from stepping out in the world and allowing yourself to truly shine. In fact, feeling you have to have the perfect body prevents you from being you — which, incidentally, is the most attractive look of all.

Conversely, you have a positive body image if you identify with the following:

- **You acknowledge that the way you look plays a very small part in how attractive you really are.**
- **You place a high value on yourself, regardless of your body shape or appearance.**
- **You feel comfortable in your own body.**
- **You accept what you look like and who you really are.**
- **You accept compliments graciously.**

If you have a positive body image you see yourself as you really are — imperfectly perfect! You recognize that although you may not meet the ideals of the media or society (let's face it — who actually does?) you still feel generally happy with the way you look. As a result, this body-confident mindset leads to increased self-confidence, self-value and self-worth.

Take a minute to ponder how you view your own body. Can you

actually say out loud that you like it? Are there any particular body parts you do like? What are the parts that you feel ashamed of or wish could be different? Would you like to have a different attitude about your body? How different do you think your life would be if you could just accept that your body is part of who you are and in fact, it is what makes you unique? How good would it feel if, rather than trying so hard to be like other people, you simply decided to be yourself and accept your body the way it is?

We often fail to realize that a healthy body image is nothing more than a realistic body image. It is about acknowledging and respecting your unique natural body shape, as nature intended it to be. Okay, you may not be a supermodel or male pin-up material but that doesn't mean that your body shape is wrong in any way or that you are flawed or less worthy of acceptance than other people.

Regardless of where we come from or what sex we are, each and every one of us has our own size, colour and shape. Look around you — doesn't everyone on the planet have a unique body shape? Isn't it perfectly normal if your nose, hair or body shape is different from that of other people? So, considering this uniqueness, why do we assume that we have to meet a particular style or shape in order to be viewed as 'attractive'?

Supermodels only represent a miniscule percentage of the population, and the images we see of both male and female celebrities are all digitally enhanced and airbrushed anyway. Let's look at the animal kingdom: isn't it normal that every animal has a different shape and size? Don't we just accept this and love them for their differences? Imagine if we decided that all animals had to look like a greyhound in order to be attractive!

Another key input into having a healthy body attitude is remembering that there is so much more to people than the way they look.

Remember, just because someone looks good does not make them a better or more valuable person than you.

TAKING BACK YOUR POWER AND BECOMING BODY CONFIDENT

In this chapter, we will now start work on helping you to build up your body confidence from the inside out.

The first step in this important process is for you to decide right now to take back your power from the misleading images that are slapped all over the media, your own negative programming or any other negative influence that could be influencing the way you feel about your body.

Remember, you always have a choice in life about how you feel about anything. So, if your body image has been getting you down, it really is time to reclaim your power, change your attitude and take some action. You alone can do this, so make a decision right now to start to feel better about the way you look. You owe it to yourself to value your body.

The fact remains that you are going to fall short of the stereotypical 'perfect' body shape. I really do find it an important step to accept and acknowledge this within yourself, because no amount of wishing things were different is going to change this fact. Indeed, spending time wishing things were different is only going to result in you feeling unmotivated and resentful. Therefore, simply acknowledging this reality may assist you in your journey to improving your body-image confidence.

> **'I resent that there is an image of perfection that is getting thinner and thinner. I hope that in some small way I'm able to say, "I'm a normal person; I'm doing all right. I've got a lovely husband and children, and I didn't lose weight to find those things, and those things are what should be important."' Kate Winslet, actor**

Let's take the time to dig into your current body-image mindset, because feeling good about yourself can only come from one place — inside you.

I know you won't believe me, but you really are amazing and beautiful. Other people can probably see it but you can't because your mind is too full of what you believe is wrong with you.

Read the above statement lines again; how do these words make you feel? Do you cringe when you read them? Does your mind become flooded with reasons why you are not amazing and beautiful and these words are not meant for you?

If so, remind yourself that these are only old negative thought patterns that don't make you feel very good. You have probably been running on these patterns for a long time, so instead of buying into them, try to soothe yourself with healthy statements such as the following:

- **It's all right that I feel this way; I know that in time I can learn to feel better about the way I look.**

- **I am looking forward to feeling better about the way I look.**

- **I know I am not perfect but hey, neither is anyone else.**

- **I know I am going to feel so much better when I can accept who I am, inside and out.**

- **I am really looking forward to feeling good about my body shape.**

- **I may not be model material, but I have so much to offer the world.**

- **I know that when I start to see myself as attractive, other people will also see me as attractive.**

Don't put pressure on yourself to find soothing words every time an automatic negative thought pops up. Just try your best and have patience with yourself. If you catch your thoughts even twice a week, then that is great progress.

MIRROR WORK

When you take a good look at yourself in the mirror, what do you see? Are your first thoughts about the size of your belly, the wrinkles, your bald head, the crow's feet on your face or the size of your muffin top?

Sadly, you are not alone. Most people focus primarily on the parts of their body that they don't like, rather than the parts of their body that they may find quite acceptable. Isn't it sad that we are experts at criticizing ourselves?

It is little wonder that so many of us avoid looking in the mirror. When was the last time you looked into the mirror and actually said something nice about your reflection?

'I used to look in the mirror and think I was so ugly that people would be laughing at me behind my back.' Lisa, 45

Before we move on, I would like you to stop, take a deep breath and give yourself permission to be a little kinder to your body — regardless of its shape, appearance or size. Don't fool yourself into thinking that you can only do this once you have lost weight, dropped a few clothing sizes or are all dressed up for a night out. If you are always waiting for that perfect moment before you feel good about your body image, you are shutting yourself off from positive thoughts and emotions for the majority of your life. I encourage you to start to focus on your body as if you were its best friend — rather than its archenemy.

ACTION STEP

> **Give yourself permission to be kinder to your body. Don't treat your body as something that needs to be constantly improved before you are prepared to treat it with kindness.**

Often we forget that our body has far more uses than just looking good. Our body is actually a powerful, intelligent mechanism that allows us to do wonderful things each day, but we rarely stop and remind ourselves of all the good things it has to offer because we are too focused on the blemishes rather than the blessings.

Learning to appreciate your body for the wonderful gifts it gives is a great way to improve your body image and begin to enjoy all the amazing things your body can do for you. For example, did you know that your skin replaces itself once a month, and your stomach lining every five days?

In the exercise below, I am going to share with you a simple way to make friends with your body, rather than feeling like your body has betrayed you with its shape or appearance.

Several times a week, look into the mirror and instead of immediately being critical and focusing on an area of your body you dislike, pick out a specific part — for example, it could be your eyes, belly or your ears.

Now, go on to thank this specific body part for the gifts it provides you with — for example, you could thank your eyes for helping you see, watch your favourite sporting team, read books, or help you to get to sleep each night. If you choose your belly, thank it for keeping your trousers up or assisting in the digestion of your food.

The idea of this exercise is that you start to create a more positive attitude about the role your body plays in your life, so don't take this process too seriously; just have some fun coming up with different ways your body helps you.

> **I spent the past forty years of my life hating my fat thighs. This self-hatred of my body had kept me wearing only long skirts and trousers, and I hardly ever went to the beach. At first when I tried this exercise, I found it really difficult — my thighs disgusted me and I didn't even want to look at them. However, in time, I started to realize that every single person on this earth has a part of their body that they don't like, so why should I be any different? I actually sat around with my friends one evening and we all shared how useful our thighs, belly and bum really were! This actually felt so good to me and we ended up having a good old giggle about how we spend most of our lives covering up the bits we didn't want other people to see. I now really appreciate my thighs because let's face it, I wouldn't be able to walk without them, would I?' Nora, 48**

TREAT YOUR BODY TO SOME LOVE

I hope that the previous exercise has started you thinking a little bit differently about what a blessing your body is. It really is more than a pretty ornament: it is the vehicle of your life.

My next challenge to you is to be willing to give your body some love.

Rather than looking in the mirror, this exercise is best carried out in the bath or shower. It is pretty simple: begin again by selecting a specific part of your body. This time, however, in addition to feeling grateful for all the wonderful things that this part allows you to do, you are also going to give your body some positive attention and love.

You could do this by massaging some nice shower gel into your legs or giving your arms a well-deserved blast of love caressing them with body oil. Maybe you could treat yourself to some aromatherapy oils or bath salts and allow your body to soak in them for ten minutes? You could also treat yourself to your favourite aftershave or body lotion and give your body some well-needed nourishment. There is no right or wrong way to do this, but your body will thank you for your attention.

QUIT COMPARING YOURSELF TO OTHER PEOPLE

I know the feeling: you have got yourself all dressed up for a night out, splashed out on some new clothes and spent hours in front of the mirror getting your appearance just right. You are feeling pretty good. Later on in the evening, however, a friend turns up looking ravishing. They have lost weight, ooze confidence and look amazing! Within minutes of their arrival, you not only doubt your outfit choice but you start on a rampage of unfavourably comparing yourself to them, letting all those positive feelings you had about yourself go right down the plughole.

Comparing yourself to other people is a bad habit. It sucks any positive emotions out of you and is particularly damaging when it results in you diminishing your own beauty.

Imagine how great it would be if, instead of feeling envious or jealous of someone else, you just decided to give that person permission to look great, feel beautiful or handsome while authentically honouring your own attractiveness and unique traits? In addition, what if you gave yourself permission to feel attractive instead of cutting yourself off from these positive emotions?

Remind yourself that everyone is different and just because someone may look great on the outside is not a reason to de-value yourself.

Look back to your list of things you like about yourself (see page 92) and remind yourself of the unique talents that you offer the world.

JUDGING OTHER PEOPLE

When it comes to appearances, we aren't just hard on ourselves; we can be equally as harsh towards other people. Many of us believe that it is okay to laugh at another person behind their back, especially about the way they look, how they may be dressed or their body weight. In my opinion, those who judge other people on their appearance are often the harshest in judging themselves. The truth is that if you are really 100 per cent happy with who you are, you would be more accepting of other people and a lot less likely to judge.

I really believe that if you take the time to compliment other people (including yourself, of course), it not only feels nice but it also builds up your confidence muscle. Paying a compliment works twofold — not only does the person who receives the compliment get to feel great, but it also leaves you feeling good for having the courage to speak up and give away this valuable gift to another person.

Why not choose to make the world a better place by complimenting other people more often, not just on how they look but on their personalities, kindness and beautiful hearts? If we could all take the time to compliment others more often, maybe we wouldn't have a world full of people with negative perceptions about themselves.

ACTION STEP

Take the time to compliment someone on something they do or the way that they look.

TOP TIPS TO BUILD BODY-IMAGE CONFIDENCE

- Have fun finding your own unique style. Look for clothes that make you feel good. Have fun and experiment with the way you look, but be careful not to let this rule your life and priorities.

- Imagine all the great things you could accomplish with the time and energy you currently spend worrying about your body and appearance.

- Stop talking to other people about what is wrong with your body, because you are only reinforcing any existing negative programming.

- Quit beating yourself up for eating that slice of cake or having a 'bad' food day. Every time you do this you send negative vibes throughout your body. It is far more beneficial to accept — and enjoy — the fact that you are going to have a slice of cake than to beat yourself up for it.

- Put a sign on your mirror that says, 'I'm beautiful inside and out'.

- If you choose to do something about getting healthy and losing weight, then commit to it. Write a weight-loss goal and visualize yourself looking and feeling healthy, happy and fabulous. Focus on how good it will feel and what you have to gain, rather than on what you need to give up in order to achieve your goal.

- Try on everything in your wardrobe and throw out or give away anything that doesn't make you feel great when you put it on. If you feel uncomfortable or unhappy in your clothes, this will only make you feel worse about your body.

CONCLUSION

A CONFIDENT LIFE

So, here we are in the final chapter. I hope by this time you are starting not only to see some changes in your levels of confidence, but you are also able to feel what a valuable and worthy human being you really are.

Confidence, whether it is speaking in public, being assertive or simply having a great relationship, all starts from inside you. If you don't do this groundwork first, you may find yourself struggling with confidence throughout your life. I liken this to putting a canoe into a fast-moving stream, and turning it upstream, against the natural current — you may just find yourself exhausted and struggling to get anywhere. It's also rather frustrating.

However, if you do some initial groundwork — setting up those firm foundations such as valuing yourself, honouring your own needs, feeling worthy and soothing your mindset into a better-feeling place — then building up your confidence muscle will seem inevitable, and far less of an effort. This approach is more like putting your canoe into that same river and letting the natural current gradually and easily take you downstream.

I truly believe that you are the driver of your own bus of life, and it is only your thoughts and mindset that prevent you from leading the confident life you truly desire. Yes, I acknowledge that some changes may take longer than others, but trust me, there is often a delicious feeling that accompanies any action you do take — whether it is simply soothing yourself into a better mindset or learning to honour your own needs for the first time.

If you have reached the end of this book and find that you are putting off doing the exercises or have avoided completing some of the action steps I have suggested, please remind yourself again that it is only old fears and programming that are keeping you stuck. Soothe yourself with thoughts such as 'I will be able to do this; I don't need to work everything out right now,' or 'It is okay to feel a little resistant; I will just make a start and see how I feel.' Remember, sometimes you need to take that first step, which could be simply deciding to put your canoe in the river!

As life goes on, and you encounter different people and situations in your life, you will probably need to dip back into selected chapters in this book to give your confidence a boost. Remember, building confidence is a lifelong process, so never get disheartened if you find your confidence levels slipping — this is perfectly normal and happens to everyone. The key thing is to accept any slippage as a natural part of life. In fact, I find that when we do lose confidence for a while, we often come back up stronger and more resilient than before.

Most of all, remember that you only have one life, it is yours and yours alone. Although others may like to tell you different, you alone are responsible and have the choice each day to either make it a fearful life, or a fabulous life.

You really do deserve the best and, of course, are as worthy as it gets!

FURTHER READING

Bourne, Edmund, PhD, *The Anxiety and Phobia Workbook*, 5th edition, New Harbinger Publications, Oakland, 2011

Engel, Beverly, *The Nice Girl Syndrome: Stop Being Manipulated and Abused — and Start Standing Up for Yourself*, Wiley, Hoboken, 2010

Ford, Debbie, *The Best Year of Your Life*, HarperOne, New York City, 2005

Hicks, Esther and Jerry, *The Astonishing Power of your Emotions*, Hay House, Carlsbad, 2007

Jeffers, Susan, *Feel the Fear and Do it Anyway*, Ballantine Books, 2006

Phillips, Lisa, *1 Minute Confidence Tips*, www.amazingcoaching.com.au, 2013

Richardson, Cheryl, *The Art of Extreme Self Care*, Hay House, Carlsbad, 2012

Ryan, Kathleen and Oestreich, Daniel K., *Driving Fear Out of the Workplace: Creating the High-Trust, High-Performance Organization*, Jossey-Bass, San Francisco, 2008

INDEX